# Learning Beyond the Walls: WhatsApp and Inclusive Education in Technical Training

Mahima

# Copyright © 2024 by Mahima

Table of Contents

# CHAPTER 1: INTRODUCTION

## 1.1 Research Area and Problem

How we experience the world today, as well as how we learn, has been significantly impacted by technology. Technology has enabled innovative solutions in many spheres of society. Companies like Uber and Airbnb use platforms to enable peer-to-peer sharing of resources, while Coursera and Khan Academy rely on technology to provide people around the world with access to educational resources. Within the philanthropic space, platforms like GoFundMe and locally, GivenGain enable social change on a larger scale.

Inclusive innovation in education is defined, especially for underserved and marginalised communities, as a novel, affordable, sustainable and accessible solution to knowledge acquisition for almost everyone. Mobile penetration in Africa has exceeded 80%, while in South Africa, nearly every household has access to a mobile phone. The Pew Research Centre (2018) has reported that roughly 9 in 10 South Africans own a mobile phone, while the 2015 General Household Survey found that nearly 80% of young people older than 16 own a mobile phone or device in South Africa. Many young people regard their mobile phone as their most valuable and indispensable asset (Sambira, 2013).

This study sought to explore how mobile technology can enhance learning for Technical Vocational and Education Training (TVET) students. The aim was to understand how mobile technology, like WhatsApp, can be used to enhance learning within a TVET context but outside the formal classroom. The solution will impact TVET leaders, students, government and employers.

Higher education and training institutions, like TVET colleges, are under increasing government scrutiny to ensure that students who graduate from these institutions are well-equipped with the necessary skills and knowledge to thrive in the fourth industrial revolution (Maseko, 2018). Governments, as well as global organisations like the United Nations Education, Scientific and Cultural Organisation (UNESCO), have raised concerns about the readiness of TVETs graduates to respond to the rapidly changing world of work through leveraging technologies.

This topic featured prominently at the 2018 UNESCO-UNEVOC two-day learning forum that was dedicated to a discussion of disruptions facing TVETs and how they will respond. The forum, titled 'Managing skills in a time of disruption' included messages from youth and the private sector, who called on TVETs to use the challenges presented by digital disruptions as opportunities.

Fresh approaches for how TVET students learn using simple, ubiquitous technology, such as mobile phones, presents an opportunity to bridge the digital divide but is also one that requires greater exploration to ensure that students and TVET colleges are well-served by the technology. The context of the research is expanded in the subsequent sections of this chapter.

South Africa has a young population; half of the country's citizens are younger than 24 years. It is estimated that by 2030, the proportion of the country's working-age population will be larger than that of the non-working age population, which presents South Africa with a unique opportunity to become an economic powerhouse (Taljaard, 2008). However, poverty and unemployment continue to threaten South Africa's long-term economic development and growth. Education has been shown to be an important foundation for economic growth (Afzal, Malik, Begum, Sarwar, & Fatima, 2012)). A strong and direct link between economic prosperity and levels of education can be found in many developed countries; the higher the level of education, the higher the income levels and the lower the levels of poverty (Brende, 2015; United Nations, 2016).

Education not only impacts the individual, but it can also have a powerful impact on an entire community (World Bank, 2018).There are many examples (supported by formal research) of how a household with no education among its members may benefit from just one member gaining access to education (Pervez, 2014). In South Africa, youth who have graduated from college have greater earning potential and are more likely to be employed than youth who have only completed matric (Statistics South Africa, 2011).

A crucial component of the pursuit of economic growth in a developing country like South Africa is the acceleration of the transition from a resource-based to a knowledge-based economy. The government, in its National Development Plan, supports this view and has called on higher education institutions to produce more highly skilled professionals. According to the Department of Higher Education and Training (2013), the definition of post-school education includes the provision of education and training for those who have completed formal schooling; those who have not completed schooling; as well as those who have never attended school.

Post-school education, therefore, has a critical role to play in helping the SA government to realise its 2030 vision to target 2.5 million student enrolments at TVET institutions. It is important to note here that TVET, as it is understood in the South African context, is the same as the definition adopted by the United Nations Educational, Scientific and Cultural Organisation: "Post-compulsory education and training., excluding degree and higher level programs delivered by further education institutions, which provides people with occupational or work-related knowledge and skills (UNESCO-UNEVOC, 2009).

From 2010 to 2015, the South African government achieved great success in increasing enrolments at TVET colleges. Within those five years, the headcount enrolment increased substantially, from 300 000 students in 2010 to 800 000 in 2015. The Minister of Higher Education, Mr Blade Nzimande, in his briefing on 'Opportunities for the Matric Class of 2016 in the Post-School Education and Training System', stressed the importance of TVET colleges for producing employable young people:

> *Indeed, TVET colleges play a very pivotal role in addressing South Africa's skills needs and cater for a wide spectrum and growing numbers of students. They offer flexible and diverse courses ranging from full qualifications to short courses, skills programmes and learnerships. Let me also say that while education is a key priority of government, we want to make technical and vocational education and training an apex of the post-school education and training. We aim to produce employable young people with high quality occupational and vocational education and training skills.* (Nzimande, 2017)

However, despite the impressive increase in student enrolments, the throughput rates at TVET institutions are weak. Successful student throughput at TVETs is vital if South Africa is to stem the tide on its high youth unemployment rate. Cloete and Butler-Adam (2012) reported that the average throughput rate at TVETs is at 20%, with some as low as 4%. The reasons for high student attrition in the post-school phase include:

- financial constraints;
- inadequate or absent career guidance at high school; and
- students' lack of preparation.

In addition, the post-school institutional environment plays an especially important role in how well students adjust to and perform in their course of study (Branson, Hofmeyr, Papier, & Needham, 2015). The poor integration of students from under-resourced communities into the post-school institutional environment results in an unsatisfactory learning experience.

Another crucial element for student success at any learning institution is access to good quality student support services and supplementary learning tools (Ntakana, 2011). However, this type of support is not available to all students, and nor do TVET institutions prioritise it. In 2008, the Department of Education (DOE) (now, Department of Higher Education and Training (DHET)) drafted and published a comprehensive Student Support Services (SSS) framework. In 2009, the framework was supported by a manual (DOE, 2008) that very clearly articulates how Student Support Services should be implemented at TVET colleges in the country:

> *[I]t is envisaged that the provision of Student Support Services at FET Colleges should be a comprehensive service that responds to the overall needs of students. Student support should be modelled in a manner that aims at developing a holistic person. Where colleges are unable to offer a particular service, referral systems must be in place.* (Department of Education Manual, 2008, p. 4)

However, despite the framework and the manual, ongoing discrepancies in rendering student support was noted in the White Paper for Post School Education and Training (DHET 2013, pp. 17-18) and while some institutions delivered numerous support services ranging from social support to job placement, others did not deliver any support services at all.

While the South African government has earmarked TVET colleges as critical institutions in addressing the high rate of youth unemployment, at the same time, it acknowledges that the sector needs innovative strategies to address some of the shortfalls within the TVET system. At the 9th Pan African TVET and FET Colleges Conference, the theme was 'Educating for Industry 4.0', and speakers listed the importance of harnessing the potential of relevant technologies to contribute to improving access, quality and inclusion in TVET and FET colleges, "Although the primary objective of technical and vocational training in Africa is to provide valuable employment for our young people, a strategic approach to skills development on the continent cannot ignore the effects of 4IR" (Pandor, 2016).

Globally, it has been recognised that technology can make a meaningful contribution to the TVET sector. The UNESCO's International Centre for Technical and Vocational Education and Training (UNEVOC) programme seeks to promote learning for the workplace and is dedicated to supporting TVETs globally. It is especially focused on the contribution of technology to learning in the TVET sector.

In partnership with the government of the Philippines and Germany, UNEVOC rolled out two technology-driven programmes to explore the efficacy and application of relevant technology in their respective TVET sectors. In Germany, the Social Augmented Learning (SAL) project in 2018 tested how augmented reality (AR), integrated with an app together with virtual reality (VR) headsets, enabled learning to be offset with printers by interacting with virtual machines and by students exploring technical processes by themselves and by collaborating with other learners. This project resulted in reduced costs as the institutions were no longer reliant on actual printing machines for teaching and helped students to develop their critical thinking skills as they could virtually explore the machines and processes on their own. In the Philippines, the Technical and Education and Skill Development Authority of the Philippines (TESDA) developed an online learning platform, which Overseas Filipino Workers (OFW) can use to develop their careers further so that they do not have to remain in manual labour for the rest of their lives (UNEVOC, 2018).

Locally, most TVET colleges are lagging in terms of technological application. However, it is clear from the two global interventions, as well as from the dialogue at the 9th Pan-African TVET and FET conference (2018), that more exploration is needed in South Africa to determine how Information and Communications Technology (ICT) can be used effectively by students and educators as the TVET programmes need to be relevant to the labour market and adequately equip young people with the skills required for the Fourth Industrial Revolution (4IR). This supported calls made earlier in 2018 at the IVETA (International Vocational Education and Training) Conference by business leaders for TVETs to onboard technology faster to remain relevant. According to Myles Thies, Director of Digital Learning Services, Eiffel Corp:

> *Artificial Intelligence is going to revolutionise the job market and with TVETS being an essential part of education in South Africa, it's vital for them to develop digital teaching strategies that meet the challenges. Over 800 000 students are enrolled at 50 TVET colleges on 264 campuses around the country and it's imperative these students remain relevant. Graduates already face an uphill battle to find employment, so they have to exit their courses with the ability to adapt to a changing work environment as quickly as possible.* (IT News, 2018)

The literature that framed this study included learning theories and mobile learning (mlearning) with a focus on mlearning interventions in emerging economies. The mlearning definition applied in this study came from the Global System for Mobile Communications (GSMA), i.e. "mlearning is the ability to access educational resources, tools and materials at anytime from anywhere, using a mobile device" (GSMA, 2010, p. 6). Mlearning students can access content on mobile phones (smart and feature phones), MP3 players, tablets, and e-readers. Mlearning can take the form of mobile apps, games, webinars, livestreams, instant messages or podcasts.

It is clear that greater exploration of the use of ICT, in general, and mlearning, in particular, in TVETs both globally and in South Africa, has become an area of burgeoning interest, yet, it is still very new:

> *The educational arena of mobile learning is still in its infancy. While there are many institutions that are offering mobile courses, an in-depth understanding of the pedagogical issues related to online education remains an unexplored frontier. Many mobile courses are nothing but web pages combined with mail and*

*chat rooms without any pedagogical foundation. There is a need to explore skill-pedagogy-technology-nexus to meet the demand of the online millennium learner.*

(Majumdar, 2018, p. 3)

The motivation to explore how mobile technology can be used to enhance learning has encouraged greater research on the topic. There is a plethora of literature covering mlearning projects and initiatives, as well as their application in education, but these reports and studies are predominantly focused on interventions in secondary education and universities. Research about mlearning within TVETs, meanwhile, is based within international contexts. The body of work available that focuses on mlearning in South African TVET colleges is limited to official government documents such as the White Paper for Post School Education and Training (DHET 2013) and the Student Support Services Framework (DOE, 2008) and the work of international bodies, such as UNESCO. Studies in the literature focused on student use of mobile technology for learning do not concentrate on South African TVET colleges.

Despite the high rate of youth unemployment and the high attrition rates at TVETs, South Africa is also home to great technological innovations. An example of this is Mxit, a South African social media network established in 2005, that had – at its peak – over 42 million users globally. In 2015, it was reported that there were 1.2 million monthly active users in South Africa, with over 60% being between the ages of 18 and 25. After the technology company closed its commercial operations, its social arm, The Reach Trust (formerly Mxit Reach), used the technology to build social and educational apps.

The WhatsApp application is reported to be the most popular social media platform amongst South African youth (Sunday Times Next Gen, 2019), and has also become a popular mobile device application for learning and teaching (Cetinkaya, 2017). This particular format of mlearning has been assessed in this case study.

The rationale for this research was based on the recognition that no current literature exists that focuses specifically on how mlearning interventions, particularly WhatsApp, can be used by students within South African TVETs to enhance their learning experience. The research is predicated on the belief that access to good quality psychosocial support, educational content and industry experts is essential for under-resourced youth to break the cycle of poverty. An enhanced learning experience that helps foster lifelong learning and builds social capital can lead to greater student engagement and throughput, which in the long term could help stem the tide of youth unemployment in South Africa.

## 1.2 Research Questions and Scope

The main research question that guided this study is:

**How can mobile technology enhance students' learning experiences in technical vocational training in South Africa?**

To best answer this question, the following sub-questions were employed:

1. What contributory factors led to the students' successful use of the mtech?
2. What factors inhibited students use of the mtech?
3. What changes would students want that would support use of mtech for learning?

A single case study was designed to explore the mlearning experiences of 50 students at one TVET institution, namely False Bay College. While the college has six campuses across the Western Cape, this research is focused on students based at one campus located at Muizenberg. This enabled the researcher to better manage her time spent at the campus, as well as the time needed to travel to the campus. The Muizenberg campus is conveniently located at the same venue as the TVET college's head office, thus allowing for easy access to the lecturers or admin staff. The researcher tried to vary the student population by working with two different groups of students. These groups comprise N4 students studying Hospitality, and N5 students who were studying Travel and Tourism. Prior to the commencement of the study, the researcher met with all the students (in a classroom setting) to explain that their participation in the study was entirely voluntary and that for those who chose to participate, no extra credit would be awarded. They were also informed that they could choose to leave the group at any time and would not be penalised in any form. The follow-up interviews with a smaller group of students were recorded and transcribed, after which the recordings were deleted. The students were given nondescript labels to protect their identities and to ensure their privacy. A limitation of this research could be that the selected interviewees did not represent the population, thus there may be concerns regarding the study's generalisability.

## 1.3 Research Assumptions

At the time of the study, the researcher was working at The Reach Trust, a Public Benefit Organisation that uses mobile technology to address some of South Africa's most pressing educational and social problems.

In 2014, the Reach Trust, in partnership with the Department of Basic Education (DBE) and the United Nations International Children's Emergency Fund (UNICEF), launched a mobile learning platform called Ukufunda, which sought to harness the potential of mlearning to contribute to improving access, quality and inclusion in secondary school education.

This research aimed to focus on student learning experiences and was strongly influenced by the researcher's work experiences in the development sector. Throughout the study, the researcher had to ensure that assumptions were bracketed when doing data collection and analysis. To mitigate this, no researcher bias was incorporated into the interview question script. Another study assumption was that the participants answered all the questions honestly.

## 1.4 Research Ethics

An Ethical Clearance form was submitted and this, together with this section, evidences sufficient consideration of the possible ethical implications of the research. A more detailed discussion of the ethical considerations of this study are given in Chapter 3.

## 1.5 Chapter Conclusion

In conclusion, this chapter serves to provide a broad overview of the study. The research topic was introduced, as were the background and significance of the study, the research questions and the context of the study. The researcher's focus was on understanding how mobile technology can enhance learning at a TVET college. Chapter 2 presents the literature review, which covers mobile learning and the learning theory that framed the study; Chapter 3 presents the research methodology employed in the study; Chapter 4 covers the findings and analysis; and Chapter 5 discusses the study's contribution to the literature.

# CHAPTER 2: LITERATURE REVIEW

## 2.1. Introduction

Professor Sugata Mitara's words are even more relevant today than in 2012 when he shared these words in a short film that contemplates the future of education.

> *Knowing something is an obsolete idea, you don't actually need to know anything. You can find out at the point when you need to know it. It's the teacher's job to point young minds towards the right kind of question. The teacher doesn't need to give answers. The answers are everywhere. And we know now from years of measurements that learners who find the answers for themselves retain it better than if they're told the answer.* (Ericsson, 2012)

We live in an increasingly connected world and the global village envisaged by Marshall McLuhan in the 1960s, is now a reality. In 2018, the International Telecommunication Union (ITU) reported that more than half of the world's population is online (ITU, 2018). In the same way that we can connect with people from anywhere at any time, we can access information instantaneously thanks to our networked society. In the Knowledge Economy, knowing how to access, process, generate and communicate information is critical. How we acquire knowledge (i.e. how we learn) has changed, and in this study, as the potential of mlearning for students engaged in vocational education and training is explored it can reflect which models of learning are appropriate while discussing how mlearning itself has evolved.

This chapter commences with an overview of the literature which has focused on learning theories as they apply to education. It maps their evolution from behaviourism to constructivism and finally, connectivism. Since a constructivist approach to learning espouses the idea that learning is an active process of knowledge construction which places learners in control of their learning, it is well supported by technology-facilitated learning. Hence the discussion shifts in Section 2.3. to focus on twenty-first century skills and the role of technology-facilitated learning in this regard. Mobile learning is an example of technology-facilitated learning, and Section 2.4 unpacks what is meant by mobile learning with a summary of mobile learning literature. Particular attention is paid to mobile learning affordances – ubiquity and mobility with Section 2.4.1. including examples of mobile learning within emerging economies. Section 2.4.2. segues to national mlearning programmes to demonstrate how this is being applied to education in South Africa. The discussion in Section 2.5. then moves to an exploration of different motivational theories and how these can impact learning. Since the study focuses on youth in a post-school context, it is necessary to include a discussion of who these young people are and why their stage of life is unique, is necessary, and this is covered in Section 2.6. Finally, to better understand the context within which the study takes place, the chapter concludes with a focus on South African youth.

## 2.2 Learning Theories

What is learning? Ambrose, Bridges, DiPietro, Lovett, & Norman (2010, p. 3) define learning as "a *process* that leads to *change*, which occurs as a result of *experience* and increases the potential for improved performance and future learning" Alexander (1996, p. 89) emphasises the importance of building on prior knowledge, stating that "Truly one's knowledge base is a scaffold that supports the construction of all future learning". Dewey (1929, p. 152) states that learning is an active process; learners build knowledge as they discover the world around them, "[L]earning is finding out what nobody has previously known. It is a transaction in which nature is teacher, and in which the teacher comes to knowledge and truth only through the learning of an inquiring student". From these definitions, it can be surmised that learning entails a change (in the learner), and involves the learner engaging in an activity (namely, reading, experimenting) and uses previous learning for reference (to make sense of the new). Since an understanding of learning is critical to this study, this section provides a further exploration of the various learning theories and indicates which are better suited to mlearning.

### *2.2.1 Behaviourism*

Behaviourism is one of the oldest of all learning theories, with great emphasis placed on reinforcement and repetition (Thalheimer, 2006). The latter is, of course, vital in learning; as humans, we forget information over time, as noted by Ebbinghaus' forgetting curve. Interval reinforcement using the 'spacing effect' and Thalheimer's subscription learning can aid in helping learners to remember vital information. A critique of this repetition and reinforcement cycle is that it restricts learner agency and leaves little room for exploration, instead favouring a rote-style of learning. This has its drawbacks as often the learner is unable to apply or even understand the knowledge gained (Mayer, 2002).

Pavlov and Skinner are two researchers often cited in behaviourist writings and are noted for their experiments with animals that demonstrated how negative and positive reinforcement can be used to train behaviour. The change in behaviour was regarded as learning. "The ideal of behaviourism is to eliminate coercion: to apply controls by changing the environment in such a way as to reinforce the kind of behaviour that benefits everyone" (Skinner, cited in Sobel, 1990). Pavlov and Skinner's use of stimuli to train behaviour is known as 'conditioning'. Operant conditioning is associated with Skinner, and classical conditioning is linked to Pavlov (Jarvis, Holford, & Griffin, 2004). The latter process is based on Pavlov's famous study with dogs and their responses to food and a buzzer. According to classical conditioning, a conditioned response is a response that is prompted only from the conditioned stimulus (the sound of the buzzer). The subject (the dog in the experiment) learnt to associate the conditioned stimulus with the unconditioned stimulus (food) with the same outcome (Jarvis et al., 2004). Operant conditioning meanwhile focuses on how consequences reinforce behaviour.

One critique of the behaviourist approach to learning is that it posits that the educator (teacher or lecturer) is the custodian of all information, directing how students engaged with the content. Students are rendered as passive in their own learning, only responding to external stimuli. Kohn (1999) asserts this critique of behaviourism, highlighting how the fear element of punishment for poor results or incorrect answers, further paralyses students and hampers real learning and diminishes any curiosity and learning which has become a transactional exercise based on fear.

This study seeks to explore how mobile technology enhances learning and is undertaken at a time when, as noted in the introduction to the chapter, being able to analyse, generate, work independently and communicate information are core skills. Passively receiving information is not enough. Behaviouristic notions of learning are not feasible for students today.

*2.2.2 Information processing*

Information Processing Theory postulates that instead of merely responding to external stimuli (as in behaviourism), learners actively process new information 'much like a computer', to use the educational psychologist Richard Mayer's metaphor (1996). Proponents of information processing say that the learner takes in new information from the senses, then it is acted upon/manipulated by the working memory and is then either discarded or moved to the long-term memory. Researchers have shown that there are limits to how much information is processed and that more attention is given to new information that links to existing information already stored in the long-term memory. George Miller in his 1956 seminal paper, "The magical number seven, plus or minus two: Some limits on our capacity for processing information", has asserted that the working memory can hold up to seven chunks of information, depending on the category of chunk used. This has been disputed by others, notably, Cowan (2000) who claimed the number is four in young adults. Whatever the magical number is, it is interesting to note that there is a limit to our working memory, unlike our sensory and long-term memories. To aid our short-term memories (i.e. our attention spans), Miller's (1956) research indicated that 'chunking' interrelated material helps a learner organise the new knowledge better. A chunk or unit is a shorter string of information. According to Miller (1956), the likelihood of new material being relayed to the long-term memory is higher if it can be related to information already in the long-term memory. Miller says that visual imagery helps with the recollection of information and stores it in long-term memory. An example of this is the use of a mnemonic. However, given that technology gives users access to information anytime and anywhere, and that this study explores mobile learning, a critique of the Information Processing Theory could be the emphasis placed on information retention. Would students still have to remember so much information if they could easily and quickly find it on their mobile devices?

*2.2.3 Constructivism*

Constructivism contends that learners link newly acquired information to previous and current knowledge and construct their own (subjective) version of reality. This active role played by learners in their own knowledge acquisition and construction, is best summed up by Piaget (cited in Elkind, 1968) who stated: "The principle goal of education… should be creating men and women who are creative, inventive, and discoverers, who can be critical and verify, and not accept everything they are offered"(p. 80). Kolb identified four stages that people use to transform new information and experience into knowledge: concrete experience, abstract conceptualisation, reflective observation and active experimentation (Naude, van den Bergh, & Kruger, 2014).

Constructivism lends itself well to mobile learning, as there is a greater emphasis placed on the individual's role in learning (Parsons & MacCallum, 2017). In mlearning, much has been made about the personal affordance, in that learners typically own their own mobile devices, as well as the personalised nature of the learning, that is, learners can personalise the learning based on their preferences.

Vygotsky's research stressed the role of social and cultural interactions in the learning process. This type of constructivism is referred to as social constructivism. Vygotsky also emphasised the role of the "more knowledgeable others" (MKO) in the "zone of proximal development" (ZPD) (cited in Schunk, 2012). The ZPD is the space between tasks that learners find too difficult to complete alone but who can master it with the assistance of a facilitator, coach or better-equipped peers and the tasks that learners can master on their own. In a digital environment, the "more knowledgeable others" can be peers or a facilitator. Learning is thus an active process of construction (Hung, 2001).

### 2.2.4. Social learning

Social learning theory proposes that people learn from observation of others. The main proponent of social learning is psychologist Albert Bandura who summarised learning as follows:

> *Learning would be exceedingly laborious, not to mention hazardous, if people had to rely solely on the effects of their own actions to inform them what to do. Fortunately, most human behaviour is learned observationally through modelling: from observing others one forms an idea of how new behaviours are performed, and on later occasions, this coded information serves as a guide for action.* (Bandura 1977, p. 22)

Bandura (1971) noted three models for observational learning: a live model (an actual person performing the behaviour), a verbal instruction model (descriptions of the behaviour) and a symbolic model (real or fictional character demonstrating the behaviour). In this context, 'model' is the term given for observed individuals. Two principles of social learning that are of interest are: (1) If the desired behaviour has an admired status and the model is similar to the observer, it is likely that the observer will adopt the modelled behaviour; and (2) modelled behaviour will be adopted if it results in outcomes which the observer values.

In their exploration of social learning, Salomon and Perkins (1998) distinguish six distinct definitions of social learning. Two definitions that could be of interest to this study include how individuals learn to be social learners, the example they cite is how individuals learn how and when to ask questions, and the assertion that a social entity can engage in learning in the same way an individual would learn.

Linked to this latter definition of social learning is the concept of Communities of Practice (CoP). According to Wenger (2001), Communities of Practice are formed "by people who engage in a process of collective learning in a shared domain of human endeavour... who share a concern or a passion for something they do and learn how to do it better as they interact regularly". This definition again emphasises the importance of the social aspect of learning, which enables the person to become a meaning-making entity; even if a learner does not join an activity, they can still learn by participating on the side-lines. Wenger (2010, p. 2) elaborates further on this notion of the role the of community in helping to shape the learning and thinking of each member of a community, "Learning is not just acquiring skills and information; it is becoming a certain person - a knower in a context where what it means to know is negotiated with respect to the regime of competence of a community".

Brown (2003) claims that that CoPs become the teachers or instructors for members of that community. He says that focus needs to be given to utilise better, what he calls the 'community mind' as a way to use existing learning resources, but also to accelerate learning. Since this study is focused on how an mlearning intervention enhances the learning experience amongst technical and vocational students, it may well include peer-to-peer learning and, aspects of the social learning theory may be harnessed.

*2.2.5. Connectivism*

Siemens (2005) says that 'traditional' learning theories, like behaviourism, do not account for technology-facilitated learning, and as such, only discuss learning as an internal process, i.e. happening inside a person. This ignores issues of relevancy (how do we stay relevant in a time when information is abundant, and where it is constantly changing) and technology now performs the cognitive functions such as information storage and retrieval, which were previously done by the learner. The latter argument, therefore, discounts the Information Processing Theory.

Siemens (2005) further asserts, "Learning… can reside outside of ourselves… is focused on connecting specialized information sets, and the connections that enable us to learn more are more important than our current state of knowing" (p. 3). He argues that in a networked world, knowing how to access information and make meaning quickly from the information, as well as form connections between seemingly disparate ideas, is more important than the process of learning. Our networks and the maintenance of these connections, as well as our capacity to know more versus what we currently know, and our ability to access information, are some of the core principles of connectivism and also speaks to learning in the digital age.

## 2.3 Learning in the 21st Century

Technology has dramatically impacted how we learn and experience the world today. Accessibility to and affordability of technological devices and the internet has meant that knowledge acquisition is now within reach of almost everyone and requires that people obtain new skills to thrive in a technology-mediated world (Winthrop & McGivney, 2016). Foundational literacies like numeracy and literacy are now only the starting point. The World Economic Forum (WEF) has identified a further ten character qualities and competencies, including curiosity, collaboration, creativity, leadership, adaptability and grit to the mix of skills they collectively term, '21st century skills' (WEF, 2015). Mastery of these 16 skills is essential to thrive in today's technology-mediated world.

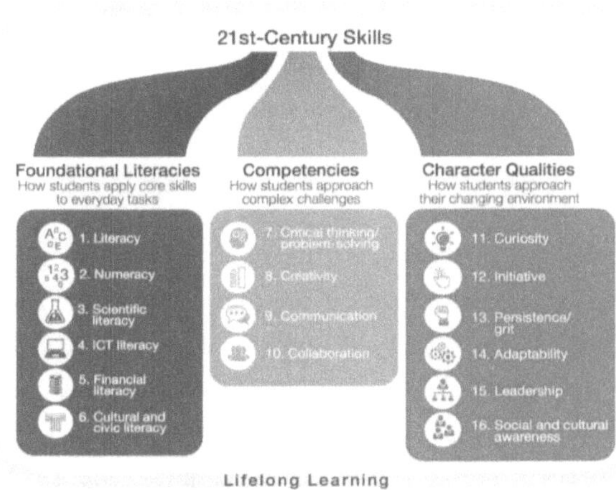


*Figure 1: The 16 skills required by students for the 21st century*

(Source: World Economic Forum, New Vision for Education, 2015)

The WEF's report (2015) also lists how educational technology (edtech) can play a significant role in helping students to develop their competencies and character qualities. However, according to the report, most edtech interventions are still primarily focused on the development of the foundational literacies. The report also found that emerging economies like South Africa, still lag behind countries like Germany and the United States across almost all skills. This is interesting because the use of technology for education is not new in South Africa. There are numerous examples of edtech programmes and projects that have been rolled out to improve foundational literacies (discussed in greater detail in Section 2.4.2). It is clear, then, that the availability of technology alone is not a good predictor of future positive educational outcomes and does not translate into a transfer of skills.

The Organisation for Economic Co-operation and Development (OECD, 2018) concurs and goes further by saying that the role of education extends beyond student job readiness and there is a need to enable them to meaningfully participate as engaged, active and responsible students.

*Future-ready students need to exercise agency, in their own education and throughout life. Agency implies a sense of responsibility to participate in the world and, in so doing, to influence people, events and circumstances for the better. Agency requires the ability to frame a guiding purpose and identify actions to achieve a goal.* (OECD, 2018, p. 4)

Agency can be realised through the development of Personalised Learning Environments (PLE) that support and motivate students and enable access to opportunities and facilitate collaboration with others. These calls for learning to be personalised and learner-centred, are not new. Sharples, Taylor, and Vavoula (2006) contend that mobile technology enables students to structure and support their learning. Lai, Yang, Chen, Ho, and Chan, (2007) describe how the benefits of mobile technology afford this structuring and support of students' learning: "Mobile technologies 'afford' real-time information whenever and wherever learners need it" (p. 328).. Mobile technology's mobility, utility and communication enables a student to have a personalised learning environment".

## 2.4 Mlearning

Most early definitions of mlearning locate its genesis in e-learning. Peng, Su, Chou, and Tsai (2009) indicate that the distinction between e-learning and mlearning remains unclear among many researchers. Mobile learning is very often seen in a complementary way to e-learning and where mobile learning is included in e-learning's scope (see Figure 2 below).

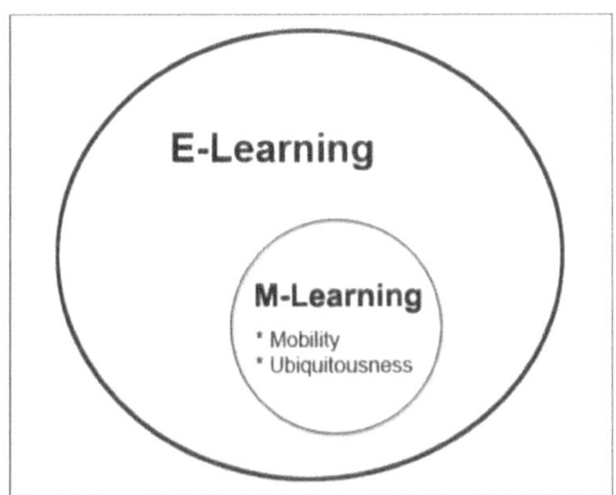

*Figure 2: The relationship between elearning and mlearning.*

(Source: Peng, et al., 2009)

Brown (2003) also supports the view that mobile learning should be seen as an extension of e-learning. However, since these early definitions, mobile learning has evolved a great deal. E-learning is still quite formal in many respects and today, to a large extent, still takes place almost exclusively in traditional learning environments like schools, higher education institutions and workplaces. E-learning is defined as, "Learning conducted via electronic media, typically on the internet" (Oxford Learner's Dictionary, n.d.).  While mlearning's genesis can be traced to e-learning, its definition must, at the same time, also include other considerations.

> *'Mobile learning' cannot merely be the conjunction of 'mobile' and 'learning'; it has always implicitly meant 'mobile e-learning' and its history and development has to be understood as both a continuation of 'conventional' e-learning and a reaction to this 'conventional' e-learning and its perceived inadequacies and limitations.* (Traxler, 2009, p. 1)

A definition of mlearning should take into account its unique mobile affordances, which include portability, collaboration, communication, interface interaction, data gathering, contextual, active learning and the outdoor environment (Parsons, Thomas, & Wishart, 2017). It is these affordances that set mlearning apart from e-learning.  This view is also supported by the mlearning definition put forward by Sharples et al., (2009, p. 5) who defined it as "the processes (both personal and public) of coming to know through exploration and conversation across multiple contexts amongst people and interactive technologies" .

Early definitions of mlearning seemed heavily-focused on the technology itself. Traxler and Kukulska-Hume (2005) stated that mlearning is defined as the use of mobile devices as the prevailing technology for education, while Quinn's definition (2000) focused on the mobility of the technology, describing mlearning as "e-learning through mobile computational devices: Palms, Windows CE machines, even your digital cell phone". This view is refuted by Kukulska-Hulme, Sharples, Mildrad, Arnedillo-Sanchez and Vavoula (2009) who state that while the mobile technology is essential, it is only one of the different types of technology and interaction employed.

Udell and Woodill (2014) have pointed out that mlearning is not e-learning on a mobile device and instead defines mlearning as "the use of mobile technology to aid in the learning, reference, or exploration of information useful to an individual at that moment or in a specific use context" (p. 6). This view of mlearning is supported by Pachler, Bachmair and Cook (2010) who contend that delivery of content on mobile devices is not an adequate descriptor, and state that greater emphasis should rather be placed on the progression of acquisition of contextual learning. Cochrane and Bateman (2010) have also argued that mlearning is different to conventional education and can provide students with learning material that is contextually relevant while making allowances for the student to stay connected to their social circles.

Yet another important consideration when discussing mlearning, is that of network and connectivity and how this can impact on learning. Sharples and Pea (2014) argue that networked technology allows learning to extend beyond the classroom and blurs the boundaries between formal and informal learning. Extending this view, Koszalka and Ntloedibe-Kuswani (2010) have also stated that, thanks to networked technology, learners are not merely passive consumers, but active "idea generators, producers of artefacts, and sharers of new knowledge through these artefacts" (p. 142).

Mlearning has been the subject of numerous research studies for more than two decades. During this time, the technology itself has changed dramatically – from the first portable Motorola cell phone in 1973 to the sophisticated smartphones sold today. Perhaps it is this constant evolution in the technology, coupled with the various applications of mlearning (from SMS trials to large scale deployment of iPads at schools) that accounts for the lack of consensus of a conclusive definition of mlearning; however, for purposes of this study, the understanding implied throughout, when referring to mlearning is that of the definition of the Global System of Mobile Communications' Association (GSMA) (2010): "mlearning is the ability to access educational resources, tools and materials at any time, from anywhere, using mobile devices" (p. 6). Of course, this presupposes that the mobile devices are networked and connected.

Fifty-four percent of the total South African population accessed the internet in 2018, 51% of which accessed it on their mobile phones (Kemp, 2018). In this networked society, new ways of learning have, and are still emerging. Rather than receiving information in a one-directional stream – as in the past – be it from the teacher, lecturer, television, or newspaper, people can now subscribe to a multitude of news websites, access research papers from scholars across the globe and sign up for courses, all using their mobile phones. By using the same technology, they are able to create and share their own content.

The table below, from Sharples et al. (2006) demonstrates the connection between how learning has evolved to keep pace with the technology now in use.

*Table 1: The confluence of learning and technology*

| New learning | New technology |
| --- | --- |
| Personalised | Personal |
| Learner centred | User centred |
| Situated | Mobile |
| Collaborative | Networked |
| Ubiquitous | Ubiquitous |
| Lifelong | Durable |

(Source: Sharples et al., 2006)

*2.4.1 Mlearning in emerging economies*

The impact of ICT, including mobile technology, in emerging economies, cannot be overstated:

*To tackle educational challenges, systemic integration of ICT has been*

*outlined as an opportunity for improving the quality of teaching and learning,*

*as well as expanding access to learning opportunities.* (Grimus, Ebner, & Holzinger,

2012, p.1)

The World Bank (2016) has reported that the Gross Domestic Product (GDP) of low-medium income nations increases by as much as 1.38% from a 10% increase in broadband penetration. Studies have shown that ICT, in general, and mobile technology and mlearning, in particular, can have great implications for the development of emerging markets. Mobile technology has enabled most countries in Africa to leapfrog the landline stage and bypass the need for expensive and extensive telecommunications infrastructure. In the period 2013 – 2017, the number of unique mobile subscribers in sub-Saharan Africa has increased exponentially. In 2013, the GSMA reported that there were 253 million unique mobile subscribers in sub-Saharan Africa and in 2017, the region had 444 million unique subscribers. Now that virtually everyone across the region has access to a mobile device, the region needs to unlock and realise the transformative potential afforded by mobile technology.

Mobile technology enables citizens in emerging economies with a unique opportunity to enhance their learning and improve their lives:

*In developing countries, mobile technologies potentially deliver education without*

*dependence on an extensive traditional communications infrastructure, leapfrogging*

*some of the intervening development phases encountered in developed countries such*

*as installing extensive electricity power grids, and building multiple computer rooms*

*in educational institutions.* (Traxler & Kukulska-Hume, 2005, p. 2)

Mobile use across sub-Saharan Africa is split between feature phones (low-end devices) and smartphones (high-end devices). The feature phone still dominates across the region, while smartphone penetration stands at 39% (GSMA, 2019).

Irrespective of the type of mobile phones in the market, it is important to note that 74% of the youth in Africa believe that their mobile is their number one asset. Of these, 63% believed the device could be used as an educational tool (GSMA, 2012). This view was still held five years later. In the 2017 Pew Research Report, 79% of sub-Saharan Africans said that the internet had a good influence on education, with most accessing the internet on their mobile phones.

The ramifications of mobile technology on education in emerging economies has enjoyed great interest from international organisations and development agencies. In 2012, the United Nations Educational, Scientific and Cultural Organisation (UNESCO) released a series of working papers on mobile learning in different regions. In their Africa and Middle East (AME) working paper, mobile learning interventions are discussed, with particular attention given to how mobile phones are integrated into the region's education systems. This qualitative review analysed secondary sources of information and triangulated using unstructured interviews. The two case studies presented were selected because the researchers felt that the projects best illustrated the potential of mobile phones to meet UNESCO's target of 'Equality For All' (UNESCO, 2012, p. 8). While admitting to a distinctly South African bias due to the location of the researchers and a proliferation of mobile learning projects in the country, the paper lists six key findings gleaned from all the case studies; one of which is that the majority of all mlearning initiatives across the region tend to be 'supply-side pilots'. This is highlighted because it is a critique that appears often in other mlearning literature, irrespective of the region (Cochrane, 2013; Traxler 2018). Other findings in the UNESCO paper show that mlearning projects across the AME region in the period 2009-2014 were typically small and urban-based, pitched at all education levels and settings (ranging from primary school to tertiary institutions) and, used predominantly text-based communication with little consideration for the implications of national policy.

The Rumie tablet is a low-cost educational tablet, described as a "library on a chip" (Northrop, 2018 p. 4) because one device can hold over 600 digital textbooks. It has been rolled out via a social startup. The Rumie Initiative targets under-resourced youth living in seven countries –

Uganda, Tanzania, Rwanda, Liberia, The Gambia, Haiti and South Africa. Each device is loaded with a collection of textbooks, reference books, exercises and quizzes which can all be updated via monthly synchronisation with the cloud. Furthermore, the device can be used offline and as all work on the tablet can be tracked, the user's progress can be monitored and evaluated. A study conducted in 2016 concluded that use of Rumie tablets across the seven implementing countries showed an improvement in students' maths and reading abilities and that there was an appetite for eduware as usage data which indicates students accessed a diverse range of educational material. Furthermore, feedback gathered from teachers and students alike indicated an overwhelmingly positive attitude towards the use of the tablets (Moon, Kavanagh, Jeffrey, Gebbels & Korsgaard, 2016).

In the Philippines, the Text2Teach programme uses mobile technology to reach teachers in rural areas or under-resourced schools. Supplementary educational material, mainly videos, is sent to the teachers' phones which they share with the students. The videos are used to enhance lessons; teachers in the programme are connected with their peers to share lesson plans, and ideas on how they integrated the videos, as well as asking for guidance and support. The Text2Teach programme is supported by the Philippine government, Nokia, Pearson, Globe telecom (a local mobile network operator), the Ayala Foundation and the UN Development programme, and has achieved good results. "Exposure to Text2Teach as an intervention leads to significantly higher learning gains in English, Math and Science at both grade levels." (Natividad, 2008, p. 4).

A more recent study by Mbukusa (2018) has explored the use of WhatsApp Messenger as a learning tool in a bachelor's degree programme at the University of Namibia. The specialisation of the course focused on teaching English as a second language. The students who participated in the study were surveyed regarding their perceptions of the use of instant messenger as a learning tool. Over the course of one academic year, the students were placed in different WhatsApp groups. The students received educational content from the researchers and could also post their own content in the groups. Communication with students usually happened outside of the classroom in an informal setting. Overall, the results were positive and showed that the students enjoyed using WhatsApp as a learning tool, and it was noted that they especially enjoyed the flexibility to communicate about their course in an informal manner. However, the students also indicated that the group was distracting at times and that during their own private study time they would be engrossed in chats with the group. The researchers concluded by stating that WhatsApp as a learning tool should be encouraged and that educational institutions should provide connectivity to enable greater access.

*2.4.2 Mobile learning in South Africa*

In South Africa, nearly every household has access to a mobile phone (ICASA, 2019). Mobile phone ownership amongst South African youth is especially high: as supported in the 2017 Pew Global Attitude Survey which showed that 75% of 18-29-year-old South Africans own a smartphone. Young people in South Africa also have a great appetite for using the internet, with 75% of South Africans between the ages of 18-29 years-old going online every day (Pew Report, 2018).

In the same report, 81% of South Africans of all ages said that increasing use of the internet for education had a good influence on the country. However, only 15% enrolled in online courses. This could be attributed to the fact that internet connectivity in South Africa is expensive. The country ranked 35th out of 49 African countries in the Research ICT Africa Mobile Pricing (RAMP) Index which rates the cost of the cheapest 1 Gigabyte (GB) of data. In South Africa, the cheapest 1GB at the time of the report (2018), was offered by Telkom and cost R29. This amount was seven times more than the cheapest 1GB in Egypt and three times the cost of 1GB in Kenya, Ghana and Nigeria. In some respects, South Africa has made great strides since its first democratic elections in 1994. More people have access to clean running water, electricity and sanitation, but its economic transition remains incomplete, and issues of poverty and unemployment loom large. Research has shown that education is a crucial determinant of participation in the labour market and that higher levels of education reduce poverty. "Living in a household where the head has attained some tertiary education reduces the average risk of poverty by about 30 percent compared to those living in households where the head has no schooling" (World Bank, 2018, p. 23).

The use of mobile technology in education has been shown to have some of the greatest impacts on learning.

*Mobile technologies 'hold the key to turning today's digital divide into digital dividends bringing equitable and quality education for all.' Notably, the development of mobile*

*technologies has opened up many possibilities in literacy and language learning.*
*Research has demonstrated mobile technology's effectiveness in improving literacy*
*performance among learners. Because mobile technology can reach a wider audience,*
*it holds the promise of transforming education for children and youth in isolated and*
*other underserved conditions.* (UNESCO, 2016, p. 50)

O'Hagan (2013) has investigated the potential offered by mobile devices to support teaching
and learning in South Africa. She explored the application and use of mobile technology to
address some of the issues within the country which is beset by an education crisis. She
described the vast uptake and use of educational applications on the Mxit platform by over 5
million subscribers, as well as the formal educational support organisation SchoolNet's use of
social media platforms to share skills and resources with teachers as evidence of an appetite
for mlearning in South Africa. Her overview included various other projects and/or
programmes that have all successfully aided mlearning in South Africa, especially at a
secondary school level:

*It is evident that not only is South Africa using mobile education but that we are more*
*than capable of producing our own contextually relevant, award winning tools. These*
*projects show the innovative use of technology to increase learners' access to expert*
*and remote tutoring, support informal learning outside the classroom, facilitate self-*
*directed learning, improve education results, accelerate distribution of low-cost*
*resources, streamline tracking and reporting, enable collaboration and skill sharing,*
*and promote equity through improved access to quality resources and teaching.*
(O'Hagan 2013, p. 58).

O'Hagan has also indicated that, at the time, mlearning was still a nascent space and policy
development was non-existent. She made an interesting remark that in the absence of an
mlearning policy in South Africa, researchers must "engage policymakers and influence

national policy" (O'Hagan, 2012, p. 58). However, despite mlearning now being a more established practice in the country, there is still no formal mlearning policy in South Africa.

Roberts, Spencer-Smith, Vänskä, and Eskelinen (2015) have reviewed the Nokia Mobile Mathematics Service in South Africa. The project aimed to measure the effectiveness of using mlearning to support mathematics performance at the secondary school level. It emerged from their research that a core group of learners used the tool regularly. These learners were not sent reminders, nor were they prompted by teachers. This indicated the degree of intrinsic motivation on the part of learners who did engage with the app. Findings of the study indicated that learner use increased over time – attributable to either user familiarity of the app and its offering or an increase in visitations due to examination preparations. It is interesting to note too that like the Namibian WhatsApp study, the learning took place in an informal context, i.e. participants typically accessed the app after school, usually at home or on their way home from school and not in the classroom.

Within the higher education sphere, a study by Viljoen, Du Preez, and Cook, (2005) tested how SMS technology supported distance education in South Africa, indicating that mlearning's success and impact is dependent on more than the technology. They acknowledged the benefits of mobile phones in supporting students but highlighted the need for a well-designed mlearning environment by capable education specialists.

Dzvapatsva, Mitrovic & Dietrich (2014) tested the use of a social media platform for the improvement of academic performance at a TVET college. Embracing the 'anytime and anywhere' aspect of mlearning, i.e. "access to the most current content and information" (WEF, 2012) the researchers tested the use of a knowledge portal to verify assessment quality (for lecturers) and also to verify social media's increase of contact time between students and lecturers to establish if it led to an improvement in test scores. The results were impressive: a 35% improvement in the academic performance of students who used the platform. An interesting discovery was that the platform afforded shy students with an anonymous channel to approach lecturers [as] 'shy students', [which] proved to have benefited [them] more online than ... through face-to-face interaction with the lecturer" (Dzvapatsva, et al., 2014, p. 3).

## 2.5 Motivation

Since this study is interested in how mobile technology enhances the learning experiences of students, literature that focused on theories of motivation were also examined to better understand what motivates students to learn. In the earlier discussion (Section 2.2) of the different learning theories, this study reveals *how* students learn; in this section, this study understands better *why* they learn.

Learning, as established earlier, takes place when students refine and expand existing skills and knowledge. This process, as discussed, involves retrieval and storage, repetition, attention and organisation. These are all closely linked to motivation. Schunk, Meece and Pintrich (2014) define motivation as "the process whereby goal-directed activity is instigated and sustained" (p. 4). Motivated students actively choose to learn, persevere despite difficult tasks, and revise their work. Motivation, therefore, engages learners in activities that facilitate learning (Schunk, 2012).

There are two types of motivation: intrinsic and extrinsic. Woollfolk (2008) defines intrinsic motivation as "motivation associated with activities that are their own reward" (p. 373). An example would be a person who engages in an activity, like a sport, because they enjoy the sporting activity and not because they want to win or are being rewarded. Using the same scenario in the example to explain extrinsic motivation, the person would, by contrast, engage in the sporting activity because they wanted to receive a reward. "Extrinsic motivation involves engaging in an activity for reasons external to the task" (Schunk, 2012).

A study examining the role of technology to motivate students in a classroom setting found that the use of technology for learning had positive effects on students and teachers alike Students reported that the use of technology in the classroom helped them to stay motivated and "gave them a strong sense of independence" (Tosuncuoglu, 2012, p. 680).

The model of motivated learning is a generic model not subscribing to a particular motivational theory, instead, it describes how motivation is linked to and evolves during learning, splitting it into three distinct phases: pre-task, during-task and post-task. Schunk (2012) asserts that there are different variables that influence students' motivation before, during and after a learning activity. Pre-task variables include goals (social and academic); expectations (self-efficacy and outcome); perceptions of value (or perceived importance of learning); affects (anxious, excited); needs and social support. Variables that influence learning during a task include instructional (teachers, equipment, material), contextual (social and environmental) and personal (knowledge construction, effort, persistence, etc.). Post task is the period after a learning activity is completed, as well as during a task when the student engages in self-reflection and includes the same variables as pre-task. However, there's an additional variable, namely attributions. Schunk (2012) further states that the pre-, during- and post-task phases are cyclical and affect future learning and motivation.

While there are many different theories of motivation, there are only two contemporary motivational theories that reflect cognitive processes, which are discussed in this section.

*2.5.1 Expectancy-Value Theory*

The above theory is rooted in Atkinson's theory of achievement motivation, which asserts that people are motivated to perform their best because they are driven by the need for achievement. Atkinson also states that the achievement behaviour is driven by either fear of failure or hope of success (Schunk, 2012).

Building on Atkinson's theory, Wigfield and Eccles (2000) have stated that the expectancy-value model of motivation is often represented as expectancy x value = motivation. In the model, they identify three constructs – ability, expectancy and achievement value constructs. The ability construct includes the learner's current conception of ability to perform a task, as well as the potential level of performance. In the example they provide, this construct would be represented by the following question: "How good are you at math?" (ability) (p. 70). The expectancy construct is understood to mean future abilities or potential, and in the given example is represented by the question: "How well do you expect to do in math this year?" (potential) (p. 70). Both Wigfield and Eccles further elaborate on expectancy by stating that their model focuses attention on the learner's own belief of their future achievement (efficacy expectations) and not on expectancy outcomes. The achievement values construct comprises different components: intrinsic value, attainment value and utility value. Intrinsic value is the enjoyment derived from completing a task; attainment value is defined as doing well on a task and utility value is focused on the value of the task for future plans (Wigfield & Eccles, 2000).

*2.5.2 Self-determination Theory*

The Theory of Self-determination is a Motivation Theory that puts forward the idea that all people have innate psychological needs of competence (feeling competent with activities), relatedness (feeling included), autonomy (a sense of control) and that if these needs are met then people will grow and function optimally (Ryan & Deci , 2000). Meeting these needs, they assert, is what sustains intrinsic motivation. The three needs they posit are part of a sub-theory of self-determination called Cognitive Evaluation Theory (CET). They further contend that intrinsic motivation is, "the inherent tendency to seek out novelty and challenges, to extend and exercise one's capacities, to explore, and to learn" (p. 70). Intrinsic motivation increases if autonomy increases.

## 2.6 Emerging Adulthood

As noted in the Pew Research Report, youth between the ages of 18 and 29 years constitute the most substantial portion of the South African population that own a smartphone and access the internet. As this study is interested in the use of mobile technology in vocational training settings, an understanding of this age group is essential, as this presents some unique features that influence how they learn, what motivates them, and what their goals are, especially concerning future careers. Arnett (2000) groups these young people in a category called 'emerging adults'.

Tanner, Arnett and Leis (2009) state that this group is unique as they straddle adolescence and adulthood. And it is this unique life phase that necessitates further inquiry into the group's attitudes toward learning and their learning styles: "At emerging adulthood, learning and development become the responsibility of the individual and prioritization of continued education and maturation requires self-directedness" (p. 34).

Expanding on this, these authors also state that there are at least five features that are common of most (not all) emerging adults: "1) the age of identity explorations, 2) the age of instability, 3) the self-focused age, 4) the age of feeling in-between, and 5) the age of possibilities" (p.36). Many emerging adults struggle during the post-school phase as they try to establish their own identity separate to that of their parents. It is also the age that many are engaged in studies and deciding on and confirming a career path. This can be a period of conflicting and challenging emotions, and this uncertainty can account for the high rate of this group's engagement in risky behaviour (alcohol, substance abuse, etc.).

Nelson and Padilla-Walker (2013) elaborate on this in their study of almost 500 college students in the United States whereby they identified three groups of emerging adults, with distinct features and characteristics such as:

*[A]n externalizing group (high levels of drinking, drug use, sexual partners, pornography use, and video game use), a poorly adjusted group (high levels of depression, anxiety, drinking, drug use, sexual partners, and low levels of self-worth), and a well-adjusted group (high levels of internal regulation of values, religious faith, and low levels of depression, anxiety, drinking, drug use, and violent video game usage).* (Nelson & Padilla-Walker, 2013, p. 67).

They found that emerging adults who fell into the externalising group also displayed high levels of internalising their problems.

Van Breda (2017) states that South African students enrolled in tertiary studies experience high levels of psychosocial vulnerability that can negatively impact their academic achievements. This, despite research showing that South African students enrolled in tertiary studies experience high levels of psychosocial vulnerability that can negatively impact their academic achievements. Sommer and Dumont (2011) define psychosocial factors as "academic motivation, self-esteem, perceived stress, academic overload, and help-seeking" (p. 386) and state in their study of 101 students that the focus in many South African tertiary institutions is almost always only on the academic performance of a student, without taking into account the psychosocial factors that can affect performance. They highlight the skills that students need to overcome these challenges. However, despite their assertion of academic-only focus, they provide suggestions that to only focus on the academic life of a student – i.e. time management, career orientation. Van Breda (2017) state that there is a strong case for the factors highlighted by Sommer and Dumont (2011) to be addressed on campus as they consider it remiss to think of challenges encountered by these emerging adults in a vacuum, i.e. only considering the academic side of a student. "Psychosocial vulnerability refers to the kinds of life challenges or adversities faced by university students that are not directly part of their studies" (p.247). Van Breda (2017) argues that to address student vulnerability effectively, consideration should be given to the development of the 'whole person'. This is especially relevant in South Africa given the country's socio-economic context and by extension, the impact on students who attend TVET colleges. Most come from under-resourced communities and so their life challenges (lack of support, abusive homes, poverty) affect their studies and attitudes towards their futures.

## 2.7 South Africa's Young Adults: 'Generation jobless'

South Africa is celebrating more than a quarter of a century of democracy and while incredible progress has been made, and despite the country's upper middle-income ranking, it remains a dual economy, with one of the highest Gini coefficients in the world (World Bank, 2018). The country is plagued by poverty and a high unemployment rate of 27% with over half of the country's citizens living below the national poverty line (World Bank, 2018).

Moreover, it is the youth who bear the brunt of this inequality. In a time when the country should be capitalising on its youth bulge, the majority of young South Africans are excluded from the economy. Amongst youth aged 15-24, the unemployment rate is 55.2% (Statistics South Africa, 2019). Youth who are neither in employment or enrolled in education or training NEETs), constitute 40.7% of all South African youth between the ages of 15-34 years (Statistics South Africa, 2019).

The cost of seeking employment is out of reach for the majority of young South Africans and in many instances, this keeps them trapped in a cycle of poverty. It costs R938 per month to search for work; these costs cover transportation, internet access, applications and agent fees, and sadly, sometimes even bribes (Graham et al., 2019)

In efforts to stem the tide on youth unemployment, the South African government launched Youth Employment Service (YES) in 2018, a programme designed to secure permanent employment for half a million young people every year. It is envisioned that YES employment hubs will be located throughout the country and act as the connection between employers and young unemployed South Africans. The YES programme incentivises business and organised labour to train and employ young people in exchange for credit toward their Broad-Based Black Economic Empowerment (BEE) scorecard. (Department of Trade & Industry, 2018).

At the launch of the programme, South Africa's President Cyril Ramaphosa, reaffirmed the government's commitment to investing in technical skills through increased support for TVET colleges. He also noted the despair amongst unemployed youth:

*Another pillar of our national effort to creating jobs for our young people was ensuring the preparation for work readiness. We need sustainable programmes that will prepare the youth for first-time employment… they need to see that future now and today, they do not want to see it yesterday [sic] or in 10 years' time.* (Khoza, 2018)

The students in this study are classified as Generation Z (Gen Z), or people born from the mid-1990s to early 2000s (Francis & Hoefel, 2018). The Gen Z Report (Fluxtrends, 2018) found that these young people hold education in high regard, "I hope that I will be well educated, that I listen to my parents. When they talk, I must listen to them, never go clubbing, never go partying until the age of maybe 18" (p.61). However, they are also despondent about their future in a country troubled by corruption, crime and poverty. Gen Z is super connected, sometimes owning more than one device, they also enjoy strong visuals and seek out opportunities to collaborate on projects and co-create experiences, music, art and so on. They are also concerned about their futures and do not trust the government to resolve the challenges in the country and are willing to step in and assist with making the changes necessary for the country to thrive. "Right now, because of, like, the government we have, well, right now I think as a country we're not gonna develop as fast as we want 'cause we've got a government that, like, is full of empty promises" (p.58).

## 2.8 Chapter Conclusion

In Chapter 2, this researcher summarised what was found in the literature regarding the research topic. Section 2.2. provides a detailed overview of different learning theories to show how learning has evolved from behaviourism to constructivism and connectivism. Noting this evolution, and how constructivism supports the acquisition of 21st century skills as well as technology-facilitated learning, the chapter then moves to a discussion of mlearning in Section 2.4. After dissecting the definition of mlearning, the next section reviews several examples of mlearning programmes and projects within emerging economies and specifically, in South Africa. This section enables a better understanding of the type of mlearning research that has already taken place in the country. It was found that while significant mlearning research has already taken place in emerging economies, especially in South Africa, it has predominantly been used in secondary education. Mlearning research in tertiary educational institutions has largely taken place within universities. However, where it was undertaken in vocational training colleges, it has not focused on the learning experience of students.

Interestingly, none of the previous studies explored student attitudes or behaviour towards mobile learning. This chapter then focuses on motivational theories and specifically on how motivation impacts learning. Section 2.5. explores Emerging Adulthood to understand the complexity of this life phase, and the challenges common to this developmental group. This section, together with Section 2.6, which looks at the plight of young South Africans, provides the background and context to this study.

In summary, a review of all relevant literature indicates that no prior research exists within South Africa that specifically explores an mlearning intervention targeted at TVET students. This study thus focused on how mobile technology can enhance students' learning experiences in technical vocational training in emerging economies.

# CHAPTER 3: METHODOLOGY

## 3.1 Introduction

This chapter provides a discussion on the research methodology used. It explains how the research was carried out, the theory used, as well as the process that was undertaken in the research.

The study's main research question explores how mobile technology, more specifically an mlearning intervention, enhances the student learning experience in technical vocational training. The sub-questions that guided the exploration looked at contributing and inhibiting factors to the successful use of mtech by students, as well as recommendations for the implementation of such an mlearning programme.

The purpose of these questions was to explore, from the students' perspectives, the practicality of mlearning programmes in TVETs, by understanding how they use an mlearning intervention, and if the use of that programme impacts their learning experience at the TVET, as well as their overall learning. Another goal of the study was to understand how they felt about using the mlearning programme.

Research methodology comprises three processes: the research design, data collection, and data analysis. The "research process onion" (Saunders, Lewis, & Thornhill, 2009) has been used to explain the research process. Each step in the research process is represented as a layer of the onion (see Figure 3) and the research is guided from the outer layer toward the inner layer.

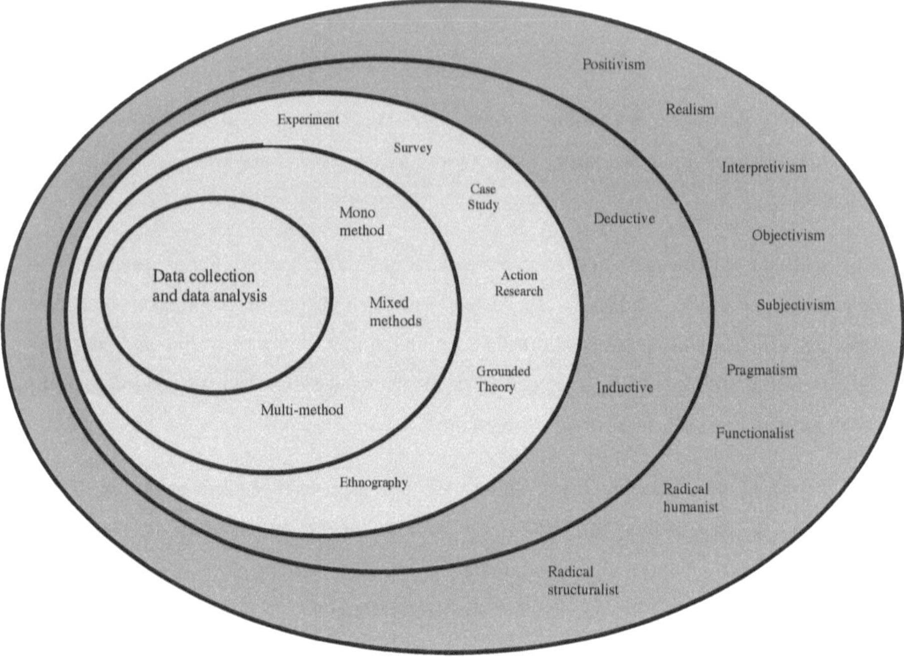


*Figure 3: The Research Onion*

(Source: Adapted from Saunders, Lewis & Thornhill, 2009)

Each of these layers are discussed in greater detail in this chapter. The chapter concludes with a discussion of the ethical considerations of the study.

## 3.2 Research Philosophy

Every researcher has a worldview (i.e. a way of seeing the world) that influences their approach to research. Guba (1990) defined 'worldview' as a "basic set of beliefs that guide action" (p. 17), while others have called it "paradigms" (Mertens, 2009), Kuhn (as cited in Schwandt 2007) defined a 'paradigm' as "a shared worldview that represents the beliefs and values in a discipline and that guides how problems are solved" (p. 183). Paradigms are underpinned by four sets of assumptions: ontology (the nature of social reality), epistemology (the theory of knowledge), axiology (ethics and value systems) and methodology (the nature of systemic inquiry) (Guba & Lincoln, 2005). These paradigms (or worldviews) influence the approach and design of a research study. In the adapted research onion illustration (Figure 3), the outer layer shows the different philosophical paradigms that exist. With regard to these paradigms, only constructivism is discussed in this study.

This study's epistemology is grounded in a constructivist research paradigm. Constructivism advances the idea that people develop meanings of their experiences and seek to understand the world in which they live and work. As the participants' views were central to the study, the researcher needed to ask open-ended questions and observe and listen intently to what the respondents did and said (Cresswell, 2018).

Embracing a constructivist viewpoint for this study, this researcher heeded the following notions:

- "Constructivists are deeply committed to the view that what we take to be objective knowledge and truth is the result of perspective. Knowledge and truth are created, not discovered by the mind" (Denzin & Lincoln, 1998, p. 7). Constructivists believe that people create their own representation of reality. In this study, this researcher was interested in what students communicated about their experiences of the mlearning intervention, as well as how they interacted in the WhatsApp chat groups.
- Meanings are constructed by human beings as they engage with the world they are interpreting. The interview questions were sufficiently broad to allow the subjectivity of the students' experiences to be expressed during the interviews, and not be restricted or influenced by the researcher's views (Creswell, 2018).
- Crotty (1998) has commented that the historical and social perspectives of people underpin how they engage with their world. In this study, a great deal of time was spent at a TVET college to help understand the context of the participants.

## 3.3 The Research Approach

The research approach of a study is informed by the philosophical perspective of the researcher, the nature of the problem being addressed, the research methods and the research design (Creswell, 2008). The approach of a study can be deductive or inductive.

As this study was guided by a constructivist philosophy, the research approach was inductive (Saunders et al., 2009). The inductive approach builds and generates theory rather than verifying it, which the deductive approach does. Inductive reasoning begins with the observation of a specific phenomenon, event or group of people (the sample) to draw conclusions about the population (Leedy & Ormrod, 2018). Furthermore, for research using inductive reasoning, context matters. "Research using an inductive approach is likely to be particularly concerned with the context in which such events were taking place" (Saunders et al, 2009, p. 126).

In Chapter 1, it was noted that no theory informed this study, as it was based on experience and the researcher's observation that the mlearning community had not yet explored mlearning in South Africa's TVET colleges. The inquiry started with questions regarding how mobile technology and mobile learning can be utilised to enhance learning experiences. The study's approach was, therefore, inductive in its reasoning; it used a 'bottom-up' approach, i.e. it started with questions before collecting data and then building a theory. "When researchers take an inductive approach, they start with a set of observations and then they move from those particular experiences to a more general set of propositions about those experiences. In other words, they move from data to theory, or from the specific to the general" (Open Textbook Library, 2012, p. 19).

Given that this study explored the mlearning experiences of students, a research approach utilising quantitative methods would not have been suitable. This study was not concerned with measuring how many students used an mlearning programme or by how much the mlearning intervention improved their results. Therefore, a qualitative approach was considered the most suitable. This need to understand the students' lived experiences aligns with Merriam's (2009) description of qualitative researchers as being "interested in understanding how people interpret their experiences, how they construct their worlds, and what meaning they attribute to their experiences" (p. 13). For this study, understanding mlearning from the viewpoint of college students meant that data needed to be gathered from the lived experiences of actual TVET students based at one college. Stake (2010) has explained this characteristic of qualitative methods as follows: "The purpose of qualitative research is usually not to reach general social science understandings but understandings about a particular situation. By understanding better, the complexity of the situation, we should contribute to setting policy and professional practice" (p. 65).

Merriam & Tisdell (2016) have further elaborated on the nature of a qualitative study by stating that it has four main characteristics:

- Gathering meaning and understanding for how people make sense of their lives and interpret their experiences, with particular focus on the study participants' experiences, rather than the researcher's.
- Collecting and analysing data are primarily done by the researcher (here Merriam noted that there are inherent shortcomings and biases but that these are accounted for rather than eliminated).
- It is an inductive process.
- It offers a rich description of the study through the use of quotes and excerpts from interviews, field notes and documents (pp. 15-17).

In this study, the researcher worked closely with TVET students to better understand who they are, what meaning they ascribe to being TVET students, and how this relates to their learning, and especially their use and experience of mobile technology for learning. The researcher was guided by questions around technology use for learning enhancement specifically in the TVET college environment. These questions then guided the data collection and analysis process undertaken. Finally, in Chapter 4, the findings provide a rich account of mlearning in one TVET college, which is bolstered through the use of quotes from the students.

*3.3.1 Research strategy*

A research strategy is a plan for how a researcher will answer the research questions and meet the study's objectives (Saunders et al., 2013 2009). Different types of research strategies can be employed by a researcher (see Figure 3), but only this study's strategy is presented here.

This research study adopted a case study strategy. Yin (2009) advised that case studies should be used for "how" and "why" types of research questions, where the researcher does not have control over the behaviour of those involved in the study and seeks to examine real-life contexts and phenomenon. Case studies are a common research method in the social sciences, noted

Yin (2009), because they "contribute(s) to our knowledge of individual, group, organisational, social, political and related phenomena" (p. 4).

This inquiry employed techniques based on the definition of a case study as proposed by Merriam (2009) and Creswell (2018). For Merriam (2009), a case study is "an intensive, holistic description and analysis of a bounded phenomenon such as a program, an institution, a person, a process, or a social unit" (p. 10). Creswell's (2018) definition of case study research, while detailed, is also the clearest: "Case study research is a qualitative approach in which the investigator explores a bounded system (a case) or multiple bounded systems (cases) over time through detailed, in-depth data collection involving multiples sources of information (e.g. observations, interviews, audio-visual material, and documents and reports), and reports a case description and case-based themes" (p. 97).

For Yin (1994), a 'case', also known as the unit of analysis, characterises research as a 'case study' and differentiates it from other types of qualitative research. Defining and bounding the case at the outset is a critical part of (Harrison, Birks, Franklin & Mills, 2017) designing a case study as it directs and frames the data collection and analysis. A useful guide in determining the unit of analysis is the detailed explanation by Stake (2005) of what a case is:

*A case is a noun, a thing, an entity; it is seldom a verb, a participle, a functioning. Schools may be our cases – real things that are easy to visualize... Training modules may be our cases – amorphous and abstract, but still things, whereas 'training' is not. Nurses may be our cases; we usually do not define 'nursing activity' as the case. 'Managing', 'becoming effective', 'giving birth', and 'voting' are examples of functioning, not entities we are likely to identify as cases. For our cases, we may select 'managers', 'production sites', 'labour and delivery rooms', or 'training sessions for voters'. With these cases we find opportunities to examine our functioning, but the functioning is not the case.* (Stake, 2005, p. 1)

In this study, this researcher aims to say something about how mobile technology can enhance learning for students at the TVET college, bearing in mind their motivations, aspirations and personal contexts (most came from impoverished communities).

In addition to having a clearly defined unit of analysis, the other unique elements of a case study are that it is studied in context (a real-life setting) and it has multiple sources of evidence (Merriam, 2009; Stake, 2005; Yin, 2009). In this qualitative study, observation and unstructured and semi-structured interviews were utilised as data gathering tools. The context of this case study is described in greater detail later in the chapter.

After clearly defining the case of the study, a researcher must determine the type of case study that will be conducted. Different types of case studies were categorised and labelled differently by Yin (1994) and Stake (2005). As the purpose of this study was to explore the use of mobile technology by N4 Hospitality and N5 Travel and Tourism students at False Bay TVET College, the study was exploratory.

Yin (2009) also differentiated between single and multiple case studies. He suggested that a single case study design is utilised when a single group or single thing is being studied, or if replication is not possible. If a multiple case design is adopted, the researcher must replicate the case, making most multiple case studies expensive and time-consuming. Researchers also employ a single case study design if the case is testing (confirming or challenging) a well-formulated theory, represents unique circumstances or is revelatory in terms of provision of access to a phenomenon that was inaccessible before. The present study is a single case design, with False Bay TVET college being the case.

## 3.4 Participants, Gaining Access and Context

### 3.4.1 Selection of the participants

The main research question is: 'How can mobile technology enhance the student learning experience in technical vocational training in emerging economies?' It was not feasible to study every TVET institution and interview every TVET student due to the researcher's limited resources (time and money), which is why Saunders et al. (2009) commented that there is almost always a need to sample respondents for any investigation. In order to decide what, where, when and whom to observe and interview participants had to be selected (Merriam &

Tisdell, 2016). In qualitative studies, there are three main types of sampling: purposive, quota and snowball sampling (Gentles, Charles, Ploeg, & McKibbon, 2015). For this study, purposive sampling was used.

The purposive sampling technique, also known as judgment sampling, is the deliberate selection of a participant due to the qualities that a participant possesses (Etikan, Musa, & Alkassim, 2016). In the present study, the participants were selected through purposive sampling. The participants of the current study were selected on the basis that they would yield rich data regarding mlearning (Leedy & Ormrod, 2018). As noted, the participants were students from False Bay College who were studying either N4 Hospitality or N5 Travel and Tourism. These students were selected because the management at False Bay TVET felt that as their lecturers already used technology in the classroom, the students would feel comfortable using an mlearning programme on their phones. The main objective of the purposive sampling technique is to produce a sample that can be logically assumed to be representative of the population (Lavrakas, 2008). The students in these two classes were the researcher's information sources, and via observation of their activities in the WhatsApp groups, they assisted in answering the research questions. A smaller sample was needed for the semi-structured interviews, for which the researcher employed convenience sampling. This type of sampling, also known as accidental or haphazard sampling, is used when members of the population meet certain criteria (Etikan, et al., 2016, p.2). In this study, these members were N4 Hospitality and N5 Travel and Tourism students at the Muizenberg campus of False Bay TVET, who had participated in the mlearning intervention and were available and willing to be interviewed.

### 3.4.2 Gaining access to the participants

The researcher initially considered selecting a sample of colleges across three provinces in South Africa (Western Cape, Eastern Cape and Gauteng), but after careful consideration of the impact on her work and family commitments, as well as the expenses that would be incurred for such a study (the researcher was based in the Western Cape at the time), she narrowed her focus to TVETs based in the Western Cape. The researcher contacted the Acting Director of the Department of Higher Education and Training (DHET), who at the time was responsible for the Western Cape and Northern Cape DHET regional offices, to discuss the purpose of the research and to seek assistance in determining a shortlist of colleges with which she could work. This shortlist needed to fulfil the following criteria: (1) have at least one campus located close to her place of work so that it was easy to access; (2) be open to exploring the use of mobile technology by a group of students; and (3) run a functional TVET.

The Acting Director expressed great interest in the study and after the initial meeting introduced the researcher to the heads of three different colleges: Northlink, College of Cape Town, and False Bay College. In the meeting, the Acting Director indicated that these three colleges were the most advanced in terms of the use of e-learning and added that she felt that these TVETs would be a good fit for the study. In her correspondence to the college heads, the Acting Director described the research focus and asked the colleges that were interested in working with the researcher to fill in and return the relevant research application documentation needed for such a study.

False Bay College's management team responded first and requested a copy of the researcher's MPhil proposal for consideration, which was duly sent. This was followed by a meeting with the then Deputy Principal of the college, who granted permission to proceed with the research and introduced the researcher to her team, notably the E-Learning Developer, with whom the researcher worked closely throughout the research. After an internal discussion, it was agreed that the researcher could work with the Hospitality and Travel and Tourism students. The researcher met with the lecturers of the two classes to share her research proposal and to discuss what the study would entail. When the researcher mentioned the focus of her study, the two lecturers were very animated and expressed eagerness to participate and learn from the findings. Both lecturers then shared how they had tried to incorporate technology into their teaching, and interestingly one lecturer had already started a WhatsApp class group to communicate with students.

After this meeting, this researcher presented the research study to the students in the two classes. After describing the aim and process of the study, they were invited to participate in the research. Students were assured that participation in the group was voluntary, and participation or non-participation would not influence their grades or prejudice them in any way. The students who wished to participate had to complete a questionnaire to establish the demographic details of the group which would participate in the study. The questionnaire provided the researcher with baseline data regarding students' use of mobile technology, their aspirations post-college, daily commuting behaviour and the distance they lived from campus. This was anonymous. On a separate sheet, they shared their mobile numbers and signature, to confirm their participation in the study and to grant permission for the researcher to use and store their mobile number for research purposes (by adding them to the WhatsApp groups). Students were also advised that they could leave and re-join the WhatsApp group at any time during the study. Across the two classes, a total of fifty students signed up to participate in the study and join the WhatsApp groups. Each class had its own WhatsApp group. After the WhatsApp group intervention and observation, interviews with seven of the students were conducted at venues that were convenient for the students. All the students interviewed did so voluntarily.

False Bay TVET College has six campuses across the Western Cape and has recently also introduced distance learning. The head office is located at the Muizenberg campus. This research focused on how students at this TVET college experienced learning via mtech.

### 3.4.3 Context

The Oxford Dictionary defines context as "the circumstances that form the setting for an event, statement, or idea, and in terms of which it can be fully understood." The contextual circumstances of this study included a TVET college located in the beachside suburb of Muizenberg in Cape Town. This campus of the False Bay TVET College is conveniently located on the main road and is easily accessible by public transport (bus, taxi and train). It is a modern campus boasting a computer lab and an on-site training restaurant. The campus also houses the college's head office and is its hospitality training hub. On all the occasions that the researcher visited the campus, the atmosphere was welcoming, and the culture was supportive and student-centric; the researcher would often see lecturers engaging with students in their classrooms during breaks. The majority of the students who participated in the study came from impoverished communities located more than 20 kilometres away and spent up to three hours a day commuting between their homes and the campus. In this study, the observations of online behaviour took place in the WhatsApp group chats, the unstructured interviews took place at the campus, while the semi-structured interviews took place at locations determined to be convenient to the participants.

Before the observation period, the researcher visited the campus to meet with the management and students. This helped the researcher to understand their unique circumstances being at a TVET college (as opposed to a university) and as TVET college students, and to build a rapport with the students and staff. As noted previously, students who wished to participate in the study had to provide handwritten consent (their signatures) and complete a form anonymously that provided the researcher with background information regarding their gender, age and use of mobile technology.

When this data was collected, only 46 students completed the forms, but a further four were added to the groups by their classmates after the commencement of the mobile learning programme. These four students had been absent on the day of the researcher's presentation, which was the same day as the foundational data collection. Figure 4 below is a graphical representation of some of this data, which also adds to a better understanding of the study's context.

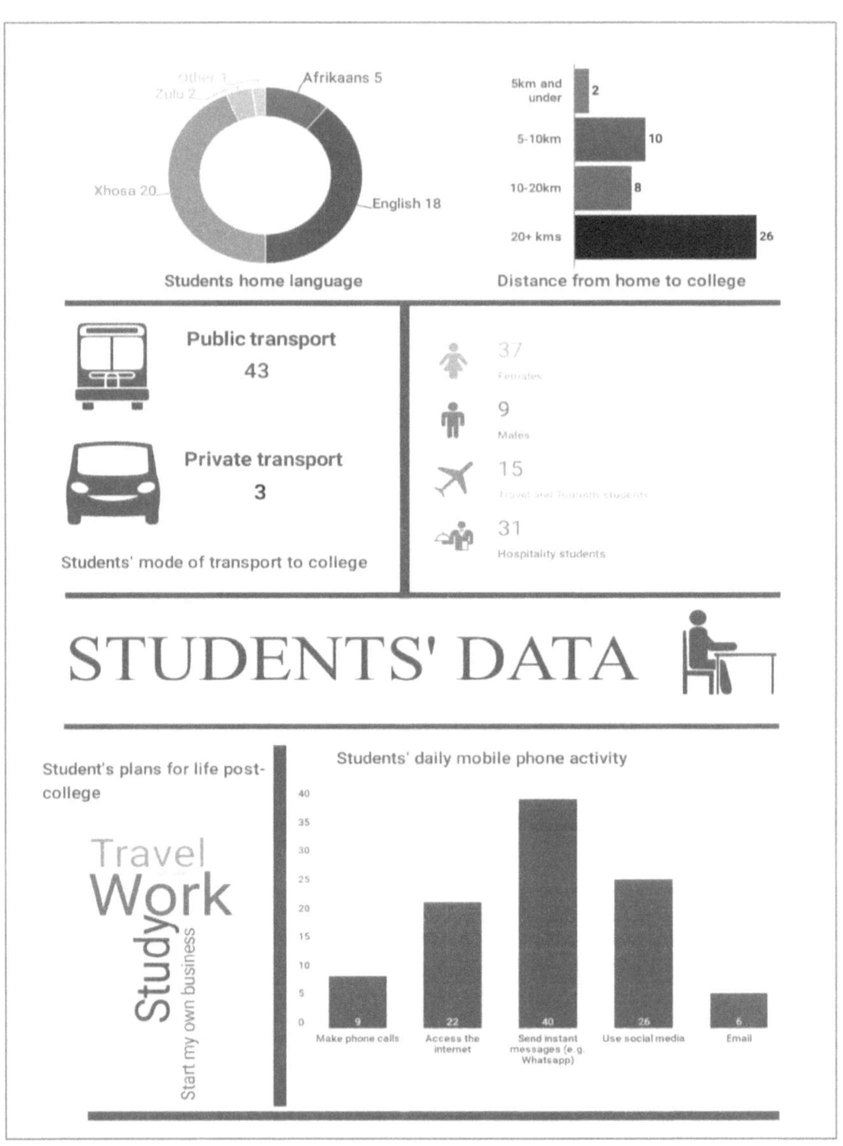



*Figure 4: A graphical representation of some of the foundational data*

(Researcher's own construct)

## 3.5 Data collection

"Data are nothing more than ordinary bits and pieces of information found in the environment. They can be concrete and measurable, as in class attendance, or invisible and difficult to measure, as in feelings" (Merriam 2016, p. 105). In qualitative case studies like this one, researchers are encouraged to collect data from more than one source to ensure that the case is described in its entirety, and so it can be used for triangulation during data analysis (Merriam, 2009, Stake, 2005; Yin, 1994). The most common data gathering instruments employed in case study research include interviews, observations, focus groups, document reviews, artefacts and archival records. How these are used depends on the purpose of the research.

In this section, the methods of data collection used are discussed. As this study is focused on the learning experiences of students using mtech, the researcher observed their online behaviour via the two WhatsApp groups. In addition to this, both unstructured and semi-structured interviews were conducted.

## 3.6 Observations of WhatsApp Groups

The first instrument used for data collection in this case study was observation. Merriam has noted that observation differentiates itself from interviews in two ways:

*First, observations take place in the setting where the phenomenon of interest*

*naturally occurs rather than a location designated for the purpose of interviewing;*

*second, observational data represent a firsthand encounter with the phenomenon*

*of interest rather than a secondhand account of the world obtained in an interview.*

(Merriam & Tisdell, 2016, p.137)

Observations are a good research instrument to use when the research question and objectives of the study focus on what people do. There are two types of observations that a researcher can make: participant observations and structured observations. The former is concerned with the meanings people attach to their actions, while the latter is concerned with the frequency of actions (Saunders et al., 2009). Delbridge and Kirkpatrick (1994, cited in Saunders et al., 2009,

p. 37) noted that participant observation implies "immersion [by the researcher] in the research setting, with the objective of sharing in peoples' lives while attempting to learn their symbolic world".

The role that a participant-observer plays in a study can be segmented into one of four categories (Gill & Johnson, 2002): (1) complete participant, (2) complete observer, (3) observer as participant, or (4) participant as observer. The first two roles involve the researcher concealing their identity, which means that participants act authentically and do not provide conditioned responses as they would with other observers. However, ethically, this is problematic. With the 'observer as participant' and 'participant as observer' formats, the research participants are aware of the identity of the researcher. The former type of observer does not interact with the participants in activities but rather observes from a distance, while the latter is more involved with the participants and interacts with them (Saunders et al., 2013). In this study, because of the nature of the mlearning intervention, the participant as an observer was the role the researcher assumed. The students were aware of who the researcher was and understood that her role in the WhatsApp group was as an observer, as well as a facilitator.

There were 50 students in the two WhatsApp groups, who were split between the N4 Hospitality students and the N5 Travel and Tourism students. The students received daily WhatsApp messages, Monday to Friday, for a period of five months (August – December). As the aim of the study was to understand how students in technical and vocational training experience mobile technology for learning, the researcher needed to observe them in an mlearning environment, which was provided by the WhatsApp groups. In these groups, the students interacted with each other, the content and the researcher as a facilitator, and it was the observation of these interactions that helped the researcher to understand how the students used and experienced a mobile learning programme. The messages sent to the students were categorised as follows: (1) motivational posts, (2) revision content, (3) challenges, (4) industry news, and (5) subject matter expert (SME) 'Question & Answer' sessions. The categories were selected by the researcher, based on discussions with potential employers within the hospitality and tourism sectors, the deputy principal of the TVET, as well as the researcher's own experience within edtech and mlearning research.

Discussed below are brief descriptions of each message category:

## 3.7 Motivational Posts

The motivational posts comprised 'hero' posts and photographic posts with motivational text. The hero posts either featured the life story of a person who had achieved great success despite growing up in an impoverished community, or 'everyday' people who were making a positive difference in their (mostly underserved) communities. The hero stories were carefully selected so that the students could relate to the background of the chief protagonist mentioned in the story. The majority of the students in the WhatsApp groups came from impoverished communities and attended secondary schools that were under-resourced. The second type of motivational post was a motivational quote coupled with a powerful image.

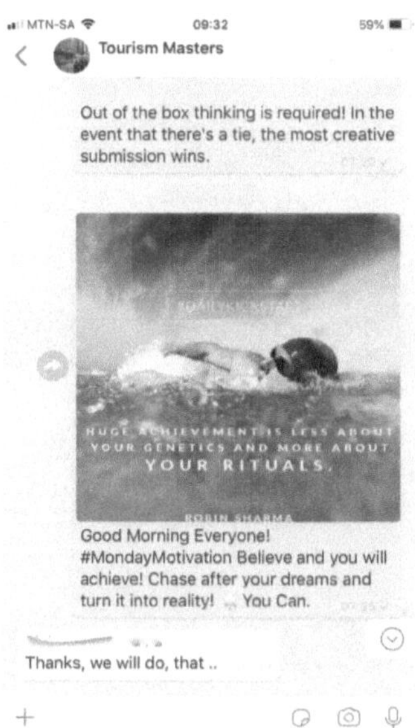


*Figure 5: Motivational post*

## 3.8 Revision Content

Revision content comprised three types of posts. The first type of revision post was based on the academic content the students were taught that day and was sent in bite-sized chunks in the afternoon, during the time it was presumed the students would be commuting. This was followed the next morning with a short quiz based on the previous day's work in class and was sent after the day's motivational post. The second type of revision content focused on the revision of past exam papers. These were sent in different formats – either short quizzes or 'flashcard' type posts, or scanned sections of the physical document (exam paper). The third type of revision content sent to students covered study techniques and tips for answering exam questions. These were sent bi-weekly, but in the two weeks prior to the exams as well as during exams these types of messages were sent every day. Below are two examples of revision posts. Figure 6 on the left was sent the morning that the Travel and Tourism students had a test that was based on those codes. Figure 7 shows the techniques for study revision.

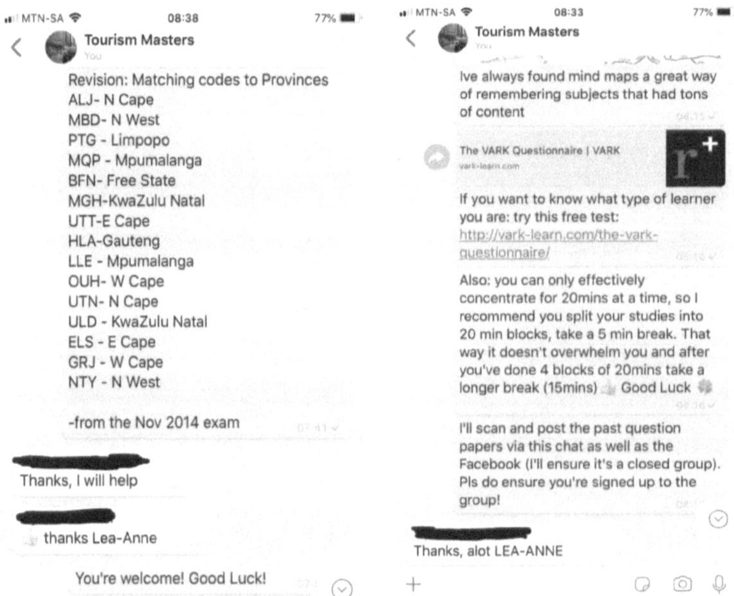



Figure 6: Revision postFigure 7: Techniques for study

## 3.9 Challenges

Students were presented with challenges aligned to curriculum-relevant content, but with real-world application. The students were incentivised with rewards for their participation in the challenge. The challenges were sent weekly or bi-weekly, depending on the nature of the challenge. Initially, the clues for the challenges were posted on Facebook and Instagram, but later that changed because of data access issues the students encountered. All the clues were then posted in the WhatsApp group chats. See Figure 8 below for an example of a challenge.

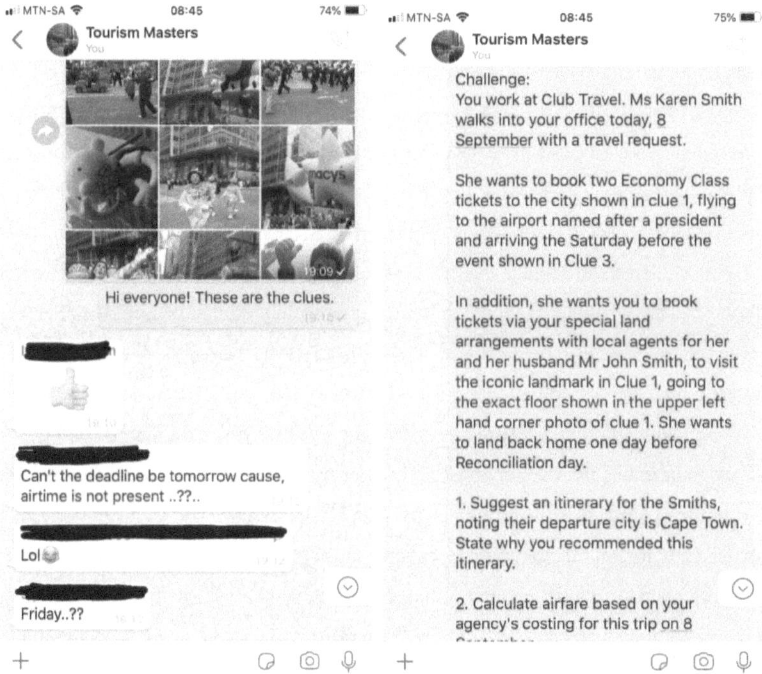


*Figure 8: Two examples of curriculum-relevant content challenge*

### 3.10 Industry News

Every week the students received real-world industry-relevant and related news. These were usually retrieved from newspaper and magazine clippings or news websites. The posts aimed to stimulate conversations amongst the students and keep them abreast of developments in their industries. The Western Cape Acting Director of the Department of Higher Education and Training (DHET), had voiced concern about the disconnect between business/workplace and TVET. She had highlighted that businesses often complained that students from TVET colleges did not understand their industry nor were ready for the demands of the workplace. The industry news messages were an attempt to assist students in better understanding the industry they would join once they graduated.

### 3.11 Subject Matter Expert (SME) Sessions

Industry experts joined the WhatsApp group chats as SMEs for 30 minutes, usually during the students' breaks, to share their experiences and tips, as well as to answer students' questions. Guests were added to the groups before the agreed time for the chat and removed after the chat ended. The guests were never told what to discuss but were briefed before the discussion, so they understood the context of the students in terms of their year of study, specialisations and interests. All the students were free to ask questions during the chats. The SME selection was based on feedback sent by students about the type of experts they wanted to access or jobs they were interested in. In the informal discussions with DHET staff, the researcher was informed that employers often complained that they were reluctant to take on TVET students as they felt that these young people were ill-prepared for the world of work. Employers noted that young people did not understand the industry well and were shy and reluctant to speak up and ask questions when they were placed in internships. The SME sessions were thus devised as a channel for students to gain access to these experts and were designed to encourage them to actively engage experts in their field and at the same time to build their networks. Below in Figure 9 are two examples of excerpts from the WhatsApp group chats with two experts.

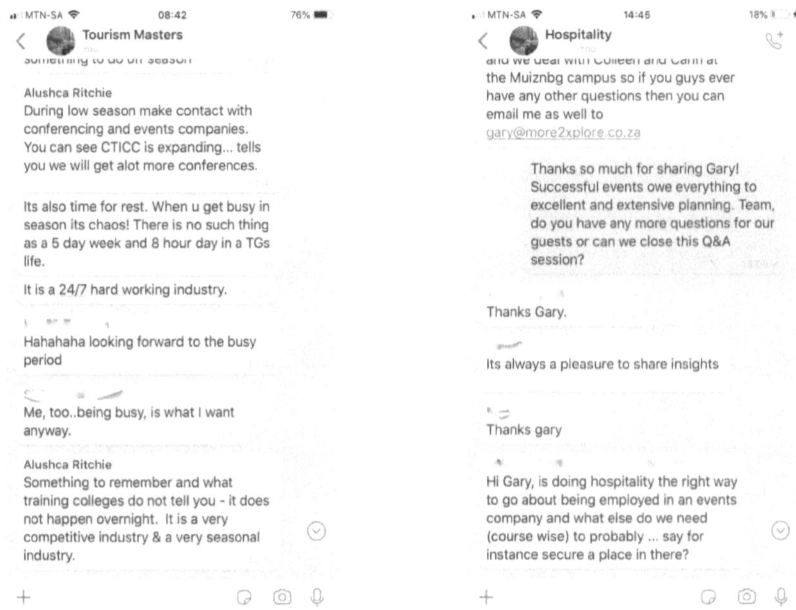



*Figure 9: Two examples of excerpts from the WhatsApp group chats with two experts*

Observation of the WhatsApp groups allowed the researcher to gather rich data regarding the students' online learning experience. During the collection of the observational data over a period of five months, themes started to surface that informed the interview guide for the semi-structured interviews.

## 3.12 Interviews

According to Gillham (2005, p. 11) "the decision to interview implies a value on personal language as data. Face-to-face interviewing may be appropriate where depth of meaning is important, and the research is primarily focused on gaining insight and understanding".

Interviewing for research is different from other types of interviews, as there is a specific structure and purpose to it (Brinkmann & Kvale, 2014). While DeMarrais & Lapan (2004, p.54) have defined an interview as "a process in which a researcher and participant engage in a conversation focused on questions related to the research study".

The semi-structured interviews conducted were preceded by observations and unstructured interviews. Both data sets helped the researcher to better understand the research and assisted with crafting the questions for the semi-structured interviews. The semi-structured interviews had to further explore students' experiences of using the WhatsApp groups: how the students' felt being connected to other students and experts, how the use of the WhatsApp groups impacted their studies and attitudes toward learning, and why they participated in the groups.

Different types of research interviews can be used, with the type selected being dependent on the amount of structure that is desired (Merriam, 2016). The most rigid type of interview is the highly structured interview, also known as a standardised interview, in which the questions, and order in which they are asked, is pre-determined. This type of interview is usually used to obtain demographic data, e.g. age, gender, education, etc. As qualitative studies are typically concerned with understanding the lived experiences of people, the rigidity of this type of survey does not allow research participants to express their understandings of the world.

The second type of interview is the semi-structured interview, which is the type of interview the researcher employed for interviewing the smaller sample of participants. Seven students participated in the semi-structured interviews. In this type of interview there is usually an 'interview guide' that is used by the interviewer. The list of questions and topics included in the guide ensure that specific data are gathered during the conversation that aligns with the study's objectives, yet while it has an order, there is flexibility within semi-structured interviews to allow the interviewer to jump between topics and questions if it makes sense to do so, based on the answers provided. The questions are flexible and there is room to probe the interviewees further with questions not listed in the guide, should interesting data emerge.

In semi-structured interviews there is no predetermined wording or order, there is greater flexibility than the structured interview, and because it does not feel as rigid as a structured interview, it is usually more relaxed with flowing conversation, enabling the interviewee to express themselves more freely. Semi-structured interviewing, according to (Bernard, 1988), is best used when a researcher is not likely to get another chance to interview someone. Semi-structured interviews tend to have open-ended questions, which allow for the interview to diverge and feel more conversational. It is thus highly recommended that these types of interviews be recorded.

These types of interviews do require more interviewing skill on the part of the interviewers, as they have to establish a rapport with the interviewees to enable a free-flowing conversation. Interviewers also need to know when it is appropriate to allow the interview to stray from the interview guide to follow interesting trajectories, but not so much that it becomes distracting and yields irrelevant data. becomes distracting

The third type of interview is the unstructured interview. This is usually exploratory and is useful when the researcher does not have enough data about the phenomenon to ask relevant questions (Merriam, 2016). This type of interview is not usually used as the sole means of data collection.

The researcher made use of semi-structured and unstructured interviews during her data collection. The latter was used during the initial phase of data gathering and helped her to build relationships with the TVET lecturers and management, as well as to generate information. The semi-structured interviews that were conducted with the students following the mlearning intervention lasted an hour each and were recorded on the Evernote mobile application. All the respondents were informed and gave their consent to be recorded. According to Saunders, et al. (2009), semi structured interviews use an interview guide but are not as restrictive as structured interviews, allowing for more follow-up questions, thus making the interview feel more conversational. (See Appendix B for this study's interview guide).

The interview questions focused on understanding how the students experienced the mlearning intervention, i.e. the WhatsApp groups. Questions were also asked to help understand which aspects of the groups contributed to an enhanced learning experience, if at all, and conversely, which features of the groups detracted from them offering an enhanced learning experience.

Certain advantages and disadvantages can be noted in respect of semi-structured interviews, for example, one of the strengths of this method is the rich data that are gathered from participants. The flexibility also allows for further (unscripted) questions or themes to be presented when interesting data surfaces. The use of questions like "Tell me more about…" and "Give me an example of…" are useful to probe interviewees to elaborate on a topic where there seems to be more that they may want to share or if clarity is needed. Semi-structured, face-to-face interviews are good for noting body language or tone that is not necessarily obvious when using other instruments like online observations (the researcher's other instrument) (Newton, 2010).

One weakness of interviewing as a data-gathering instrument is that it is time-consuming. A great deal of time and effort is spent prior to interviews, scheduling and preparing for them, and after the interviews, the transcription and analysis of the data takes a great deal of time. In preparation for every interview, the researcher practised the questions with colleagues in to ensure that she was well-equipped to handle different types of issues such as abrupt, hostile or shy interviewees. This preparation, together with her work experience (both at the Reach Trust and in the media), was invaluable. It is a challenge not to ask leading questions during an interview, so the researcher tried to offset this by reflecting on the process during and after the interviews. This concern was noted by Newton, who said:

> *Threats to the validity of this kind of interview includes the use of leading questions or the researcher's preconceived ideas influencing what is and is not worth discussing. Considering the 'live' nature of face-to-face interviewing and the complexity of language in use, it is not easy to avoid all these and other challenges.*
>
> (Newton, 2010, p. 4)

The unstructured interviews were used to gather background information regarding the use of technology at the TVET college, to learn how the lecturers tried to include technology in their teaching, and to gain a better understanding of the TVET environment and some of the challenges the institution faces, as well as some of its successes in technology utilisation. Once the WhatsApp groups were created, the researcher occasionally checked in with the lecturers and the TVET's E-Learning Developer to hear their perceptions about the mlearning intervention. Since they were not included in the WhatsApp groups, their perceptions were only based on their observations of the students in the class and without explicitly questioning the students about the programme. These casual check-ins were not structured as the lecturers indicated at the start of the study that as they were pressed for time, they could usually only spare 20 to 30 minutes for a brief discussion. These usually took place when the researcher dropped off challenge prizes at the college.

## 3.13 Data Management

*Research data management concerns the organisation of data, from its entry to the research cycle through to the dissemination and archiving of valuable results. It aims to ensure reliable verification of results, and permits new and innovative research built on existing information.* (Whyte & Tedds , 2011, p. 1).

This study made use of unstructured interviews, semi-structured interviews and observations of the two WhatsApp groups as the main instruments of data collection. After each semi-structured interview, the researcher transcribed the data and deleted it from the Evernote app. The researcher interviewed seven participants who had all volunteered to share their experiences of using the WhatsApp group for learning. All the participants were labelled 'P' and numbers were assigned to each one. As there were seven, the range was thus P1 – P7. It became clear when the researcher conducted the seventh interview that the same or similar themes were emerging from each interview. This was when she knew that no further data collection was necessary and data saturation had been reached. Merriam (2016) has explained that saturation occurs when "continued data collection produces no new information or insights into the phenomenon you are studying" (p. 199). The next phase in the research process was to analyse all the data collected.

## 3.14 Data Analysis

Merriam (1998) defined data analysis as "the process of making sense out of the data. And making sense out of data involves consolidating, reducing and interpreting what people have said and what the researcher has seen and read – it is the process of making meaning" (p. 178).

### *3.14.1 Thematic analysis*

The data collected from the interviews and observations were analysed using thematic analysis. Braun & Clarke (2006) have defined thematic analysis (TA) as "a method for systematically identifying, organising, and offering insight into patterns of meaning (themes) across a dataset"

(p. 2). Thematic analysis was selected as the method of data analysis for this study because of its simplicity and flexibility, "TA is an accessible, flexible, and increasingly popular method of qualitative data analysis. Learning to do it provides the qualitative researcher with a foundation in the basic skills needed to engage with other approaches to qualitative data analysis" (Braun & Clarke, 2012, p. 2).

The first set of data coded were the observations from the WhatsApp groups, followed by the interviews. Braun and Clarke's (2012) version of TA is comprised of six phases. Below is an outline of how these steps were applied in this study.

### 3.14.2 Data immersion

As the researcher conducted all the interviews and was a participant-observer in the WhatsApp groups, she was well-acquainted with the data. However, during this first phase, Braun and Clarke (2012) stressed the importance of the researcher further immersing themselves in the data and using this time to look at any texts and to listen to any audio recordings to try to identify if they link to the research questions. The current study's researcher downloaded all the WhatsApp messages from the two groups and placed these in tables. Subsequently, she listened to the audio files of the interviews twice before transcribing them, ensuring that she noted pauses, laughter, etc., i.e. the participants' language was not sanitised. This text was added to the text database from the WhatsApp groups. Finally, all the informal discussions with the college staff was added to this database. All the data were then read and re-read a few times and interesting phrases and words highlighted. The researcher also made notes of data that seemed to answer the research questions. This first step is important for researchers as it helps them to better engage with the data. Braun and Clarke (2012) suggested three questions that researchers should bear in mind during this first phase that will help them to engage the data critically, i.e. "...how does this participant make sense of their experiences? What assumptions do they make in interpreting their experience? What kind of world is revealed through their accounts?" (p. 5).

### 3.14.3 Initial code generation

A code is a label that captures something interesting in the data and regarded as the foundation of a study's data analysis. The researcher used a combination of latent and semantic codes because she wanted to retain the voices of the participants but also her world view. As an example, the code "enjoy the motivational quotes" are the actual words a participant used, but "the power of hope" was the researcher's interpretation of the same data and shows her worldview. The codes were then all inserted in a table along with descriptors for later reference. Below is an example of coding from the two WhatsApp groups. Emoticons sent by students were interpreted by the researcher to mean a word in the context of the chat at that time, so, for example, the fist bump was taken to mean "thanks", "you can do it" or "well done'. The students frequently used emoticons in the WhatsApp chats.

*Table 2: Codes – Frequency and Description/Context*

| Code | Frequency | Description/Context |
|---|---|---|
| 1. Do not want to fail | 8 | Students nervous about exams/tests |
| 2. Explanation helped | 6 | Peer-to-peer "tutoring" |
| 3. Enthusiastic | 50 | Positive responses to motivational posts |
| 4. No judgements here | 5 | Students encouraged to speak up |
| 5. Hard to understand | 18 | Students did not understand concepts |
| 6. Thanks guys | 2 | Thankful for support |
| 7. Study-life balance | 25 | Little time to revise |
| 8. Silly questions | 8 | Students, especially in hospitality, were shy to ask a question |
| 9. Want to win prizes | 11 | Expressed interest in winning challenges for the prizes |

## 3.15 Theme Generation

In this phase, all the codes were reviewed, and similarities were noted between codes. Where it made sense, codes were grouped, and themes began to be generated. Braun and Clarke (2012) have explained that a theme "captures something important about the data in relation to the research question, and represents some level of *patterned* response or meaning within the data set" (Braun and Clarke, 2006, p. 6).

### *3.15.1 Theme revision and refinement*

During this phase, the themes were checked against extracts from the data. The researcher found the following questions suggested by Braun and Clarke (2012, p. 9) especially useful to check that the proposed themes worked with the data set: "What is the quality of this theme? What are the boundaries of this theme?". Some of the themes collapsed and others were removed. Subsequently, the themes were re-read and then checked against the whole data set. Braun and Clarke (2006) stressed that researchers, who use their version of TA, see the process as recursive, and are open to some themes and codes being removed and even changed if it makes sense in the greater scheme of the study and its data set.

### *3.15.2 Theme definition*

The next step required the researcher to begin to name themes, thus she noted which participant quotes best explained a theme. Braun and Clarke (2012) say that the aim of this last theme distillation is "identify the 'essence' of what each theme is about."

## 3.16 Report Writing

The themes the researcher chose are explained in greater detail in Chapter 4. Extracts from the data are included in that chapter to give the reader a greater understanding of the essence of each theme, using the participants' own words.

## 3.17 Validation

Maxwell (2013) said of validity that, "it depends on the relationship of your conclusions to reality, and no methods can completely assure you have captured this" (p.121). While absolute

objectivity in qualitative studies is impossible, researchers can employ strategies to ensure that the findings they present are credible. Noting the importance of the utilisation of strategies to ensure research credibility, Wolcott (2005, p. 60) stated that it increases "the correspondence between research and the real world". In this study, triangulation and member checks were employed to establish the study's validity (Merriam, 2016). For triangulation, three different methods of data collection were employed, i.e. observation of participants in the WhatsApp groups, semi-structured interviews of students, and unstructured interviews of lecturers and TVET and DHET management, to check for common themes that supported the phenomenon. Member checks entailed sharing the preliminary research findings with the participants to check with them whether the researcher's interpretations were accurate (Merriam, 2016). According to Maxwell (2013), member checks are:

> *[T]he single most important way of ruling out the possibility of misrepresenting the meaning of what participants say and do and the perspective they have on what is going on, as well as an important way of identifying your biases and misunderstandings of what you observed.* (Maxwell, 2013, p.126-127).

Other strategies included reflexivity, which entailed the researcher keeping a journal throughout the study and noting her reflections on the study, especially regarding what was being done in the study, as well as why the research was being done.

## 3.18 Ethical Considerations

Cooper and Schindler (2006) have defined ethics as the "norms or standards of behaviour that guide moral choices about our behaviour and our relationships with others" (p. 116). In research, ethics relates to how the research design, data management, analysis and reporting of findings are handled by the researcher.

This study's purpose was to explore the use of mobile technology by Hospitality and Travel and Tourism students at False Bay TVET College. This exploratory case study involved human

participants (students and SMEs) who utilised their mobile phones to access the mlearning programme on WhatsApp. While this enabled observation of the participants, it may also have been seen as an invasion of their privacy. The research design needed to take into account the possible effects this mlearning intervention could have on their lives, so it was devised to cause no harm. At the start of the WhatsApp engagement, the researcher asked that no defamatory language or material be sent to the group and that students who wished to discuss anything with the researcher could only do so in the group. Messages were only sent during the week and at times that were not anti-social, i.e. nothing was sent after 8pm so as not to disrupt the students' home lives and study times.

*3.18.2 Consent*

The TVET lecturers, management and students who participated in this study were all volunteers and could withdraw at any time, with no negative repercussions. This was made explicitly clear in all interactions and communications (the consent letter and at face-to-face meetings). Throughout the five-month study, some student participants left the WhatsApp groups, and later some asked to be added again. The researcher never checked with any students who left the group why they had left or why some asked to be added again.

*3.18.3 Biases*

The researcher managed the mlearning intervention on the WhatsApp groups and selected all the content and SMEs, so she was acutely aware that it was biased. The content development and selection were based on the researcher's mlearning research, her previous work experience at The Reach Trust, as well as the informal discussions she had with the TVET and DHET management and staff. The researcher worked hard to ensure that none of the content sent would cause harm to the students.

## 3.19 Data Storage

For the data collection of this study, the researcher received approval from the TVET and DHET staff, the students and UCT's Ethics Committee. All data collected were securely stored and only available to the researcher. All the interviewees were assigned labels to protect their identities, and after the interviews were transcribed, the audio files were deleted.

## 3.20 Chapter Conclusion

This chapter highlighted the reasons for the adoption of a single exploratory case study design to better understand how mobile learning is experienced by college students at a TVET college. In the next chapter, the data analysis, including the findings it yielded, will be discussed in detail.

## CHAPTER 4: RESEARCH FINDINGS

### 4.1. Introduction

The purpose of the case study was to explore how mobile technology can enhance learning in Technical and Vocational Education and Training colleges in a developing country such as South Africa. The researcher was specifically interested in the exploration of students' learning experiences using mobile phones, at False Bay College, a public TVET College in the Western Cape.

This chapter will report the research findings and data analysis of those findings. It is arranged according to the research questions and how it was answered after analysing the data. The main research question with three sub-questions asked are as follows:

Main question: How can mobile technology enhance students' learning experiences in technical vocational training in South Africa?

Sub questions:

(1) What contributory factors led to the students' successful use of the mtech?
(2) What factors inhibited students use of the mtech?
(3) What changes would students want that would support the use of mtech for learning?

The methodology utilised in this study was discussed in Chapter 3, including the description of how the study was conducted. In this chapter, the results from the data collection process are presented. The data collection process comprised observations and unstructured and semi-structured interviews. Thematic analysis was used to identify, code, analyse and report themes that emerged in the data. "Thematic Analysis is a method for systematically identifying, organising, and offering insight into, patterns of meaning (themes) across a dataset" (Braun & Clarke, 2006, p. 2).

## 4.2 Research Analysis

As noted in the previous chapter, the researcher's methods of data collection included observations, unstructured and semi-structured interviews. The observations of the WhatsApp groups allowed the researcher to understand how the students interacted with the content, their peers, guests (Subject Matter Experts) and the researcher, who also acted as the facilitator of the WhatsApp groups.

The semi-structured interviews took place after the observation phase was completed and allowed for greater exploration of participants' experiences using the mlearning intervention, i.e. WhatsApp groups. All semi-structured interviews were transcribed, and the text added to the study's database. The unstructured lecturer interview data was the last set of data to be added to the database.

Using thematic analysis, all data were coded, patterns identified and where it made sense, it was grouped together. Initial themes were then generated. These themes were checked again, first against extracts of data and then against the entire data set and finally, the themes were named and participant quotes that best explained a theme were highlighted and noted.

## 4.3 Results

### *Theme identification*

Following the thematic analysis, several themes were identified. In the following paragraphs, the themes that emerged from the empirical evidence (observations, semi-structured and unstructured interviews) will be discussed in greater detail, supported by screenshots and direct quotations from the WhatsApp groups and the interviews. In developing the themes, consideration was given to the study's research questions as well as the codes that emerged after analysis of all the data sets.

## 4.4 Contributory factors that led to the students' successful use of the mtech

The eight factors that emerged from the all data that best answers the question, What factors contributed to the students' successful use of mtech? were:

- competence with the technology;
- external facilitation;
- access to subject matter experts;
- enables anytime, anywhere learning;
- provides access to relevant content;
- provides motivation and support;
- social learning; and
- incentivises learning.

### *4.4.1 Competence with the technology*

During the analysis of the interviews and observations of the groups, it became clear that all students were familiar with WhatsApp, had used it before the study and felt comfortable utilising the technology. This then removed any friction of them first having to learn and understand the technology. This self-reported competence (which surfaced in the interviews) may explain why so many students were willing to participate in the study and test the use of WhatsApp for purposes linked to their studies. Before this exploratory study, for the majority of the students, their use of WhatsApp was limited to social use as these responses show:

> *I just used to use it for chats to friends and family.* **P1**

> *I basically used WhatsApp to chat to friends about social stuff.* **P5**

> *Just, like, socially to my friends and sometimes my parents.* **P2**

> *I used it to send jokes and photos.* **P3**

All the students reported in the interviews that their prior use of WhatsApp was positive, and they had positive associations with using WhatsApp and that this also contributed to less apprehension with using the technology for their learning.

> *I used WhatsApp before, so like I knew what to expect, like how these kinds of*
>
> *groups work.* **P6**

The competence of being in control of the technology and knowing how to use it also greatly added to the take-up of the WhatsApp group:

*It was simple to use.* **P3**

*And it was cool to use something that was simple. No one had to teach us how to use WhatsApp; I mean, come on, who doesn't know how to use WhatsApp?* **P2**

*My friends from high school started a WhatsApp group after we finished school, to keep in touch and tell each other about jobs. I got a lot of use out of that and decided to join this one because that one helped me.* **P5**

The researcher observed that there was an enthusiastic uptake of the WhatsApp groups by the students. This enthusiasm was gauged by the number of students in each class that opted-in to the study. The number of students that opted-in to the study was high. As noted in (Chapter 3, Section 4.3), the researcher presented the purpose of the study and explained the format of the study to students when visiting the campus. Students could then select to participate in the study by providing their name, surname, WhatsApp contact details, and needed to sign, indicating that they wished to participate in the study. The researcher explained to the students that opting-in meant they joined a WhatsApp group. At these presentations, a total of 46 students opted-in to participate in the study (see figure 4 for the student breakdown). Another four students later requested to join the WhatsApp groups (see screenshot Figure 10).

*Figure 10: Student requests to join the group after commencement of research*

Furthermore, student engagement in the groups suggested that students knew how to use the technology and felt comfortable using it to interact with the facilitator (researcher), their peers and Subject Matter Experts (SMEs). Their competence using the technology was also evident by their use of the tools- adding emojis, sending photos and sending contacts. None of the students requested that the researcher demonstrate the use of the WhatsApp tool in order for them to competently participate in the study. Motivational theories were discussed in chapter 2 to understand why students learn. One of the theories explored was that of self-determination, which asserts that competence is vital for growth and helps sustain intrinsic motivation. This competence with the technology used in the study relates to student confidence, which could explain the high engagement observed in the groups.

During the first unstructured check-in with the lecturers, one lecturer remarked that they felt the high take-up and use of the WhatsApp groups was due to student competence and familiarity with the technology:

*Well, I figured that the students would respond to this WhatsApp group because they all are always on their phones on it, chatting away to friends, sometimes even while I'm lecturing. It can be annoying, but I'm happy they use it for college work now. Everyone in the class seemed to be on this group for the study, judging from the chats in the class.* **Lecturer 1**

The student competence and familiarity using WhatsApp, and understanding how to use it, can be ascribed to prior experience of using WhatsApp for college work, as some were members of unstructured, informal groups facilitated by classmates, and others had participated in a WhatsApp group that was facilitated by their lecturer.

*Yes, before this WhatsApp group, especially when needed to discuss work, like we were staying in different areas. I stay in Hout Bay, my friend was staying in Khayelitsha and others were staying in Hanover Park, so like to communicate and discuss our schoolwork, we used WhatsApp, like to do voice notes.* **P6**

*We had a class group on WhatsApp, but it didn't work well because people didn't really chat there, so it kind of failed very quickly.* **P4**

*I have a WhatsApp group for that class but not many make use of it.* **Lecturer 2**

### *4.4.2 External facilitation*

It was interesting to note that the students who had prior experience of using WhatsApp for college work, when probed about the reasons they felt some of these groups failed, they stated that it was because those groups lacked structure and a dedicated person to drive the engagement. Students who had previous disappointing experiences with other college WhatsApp groups before this study listed external facilitation as the reason they joined this WhatsApp group and participated in discussions:

> *I was, like, very excited when I heard about this (group) because I struggled in class and I thought that this would be able to help me more than the other group because there was a facilitator to look after it and push us.*  **P4**

One lecturer also commented on the role of the external facilitator being key to the successful take-up and use of the WhatsApp group during one of the unstructured lecturer interviews:

> *I'm happy to see it's progressing so well, and I was surprised that so many students joined the group. I also started one for the class a while back, but not everyone joined that one. Maybe some of the students didn't want to join it because I'm their lecturer, and also maybe because I only used it to send them homework or tasks. Also, I didn't communicate every day with them, like in this group they receive message every day, so in turn, I've heard so much about the group every day.*
> **Lecturer 2**

During the five-month observation period, the researcher who also acted as a facilitator of the groups noticed that students felt comfortable conversing with the external facilitator, and perhaps that level of trust was given because the facilitator did not formally represent the college, as a lecturer would. The students also understood that the external facilitator and their participation in the WhatsApp groups did not influence their marks or academic results.

### 4.4.3 Access to Subject Matter Experts (SMEs)

A prominent theme that emerged from student and lecturer interviews, as well as observations by the researcher, was that the WhatsApp groups provided students with access to industry Subject Matter Experts (SMEs), which was highly valued by the students.

The Hospitality students had not been exposed to SMEs in their course while the Tourism students had limited interaction: one visit from the owner of a local tourist shop who discussed sales. The Tourism students had undertaken an excursion to the airport arranged by the college, which served to frustrate rather than inspire or inform them. The lecturers advised students that they could not engage any airport staff. The students watched the check-in process from a distance. They also researched the core business of each retailer (list on a form what each retailer sold). Given this resource-constrained context, students battled to understand their field of study.

Students relished the opportunity to engage with SMEs via the WhatsApp group as they could provide real-world context and answer the questions they had concerning their respective fields of study. During the interviews, many students commented on the high calibre of experts, and how useful these engagements were in aiding their understanding of their coursework:

*The level of people that spoke to us was high. Like they were owners of companies or worked in a space we wanted to go into. And they gave us real advice. Good stuff we didn't learn about in class.* **P1**

*It was great! It was always interesting, and these people were great. Like some of these people we wouldn't otherwise have access to and here they were just chatting to us on the group like other classmates. Some of our work-based experience wasn't great and in places where we were supposed to be learning, we didn't we just were there to pass time or fill some vacancy and some of the people didn't even treat us right but here these people who held high positions they treated us like normal.* **P3**

*Yhoh! I loved this! I tried to get hold of some experts on my own using LinkedIn and at these career fares, but I didn't have luck, they just ignored me. That always sucks, because we're just students, so what can we offer them? I always feel we get looked down on as TVET students, like because it's not university. But in this group,*

*I didn't feel scared to approach because of rejection, like they just answered our*

*questions fully and completely, like they didn't give one-word answers like happens*

*in real life. They think we're dumb or rank low, so they just give a quick answer.*

*But in this group, they took time to answer and stayed longer than we agreed, it*

*was nice man, it's always nice to hear what an expert says about your future career.*

**P4**

*That was very great because like we never had that in our class and plus they would*

*chat to us like we were their equals, sometimes in class it can feel formal if we have*

*someone stand in front. Now they were like just like anyone else on the phone, in*

*our WhatsApp group. It was also so easy and interesting to follow the conversation.*

*We asked you to ask them to chat during our breaks and that helped because we'd*

*like all sit at a table together, have our snack or lunch and be on our phones, all*

*chatting to this guest. They shared so much insights that we didn't have before then,*

*like about the industry. They opened our eyes to new stuff. And it was also - ja, no*

*effort and didn't feel forced or awkward.* **P5**

One interview participant shared how, after using the group for a few weeks, she and a group
of classmates devised a plan to derive even greater value from the SME sessions:

*With this WhatsApp group we knew we were getting good stuff from these experts,*

*so we like all got together before the chat happened. We'd write the questions down*

*before we go and ask on the group. So we'd make sure that all the questions we*

*wanted answers to, we got, not like random questions.* **P7**

The researcher also observed the popularity of the SME sessions amongst students. SME
sessions enjoyed high student engagement; students seemed well-prepared and needed minimal
prompting to engage the guest. Students who either did not engage much or at all with other
WhatsApp posts would often send the most questions to SMEs.

Common phrases used by students in the WhatsApp groups either ahead of or after the SME sessions included, "excited", "can't wait", "useful", "helpful", which all indicate the high value the students assigned to these chats. Below are WhatsApp excerpts of some of the students' comments pre and post-SME chats (shown in Table 3), as well as screenshots (Figure 11) that illustrate the high level of student engagement with experts.

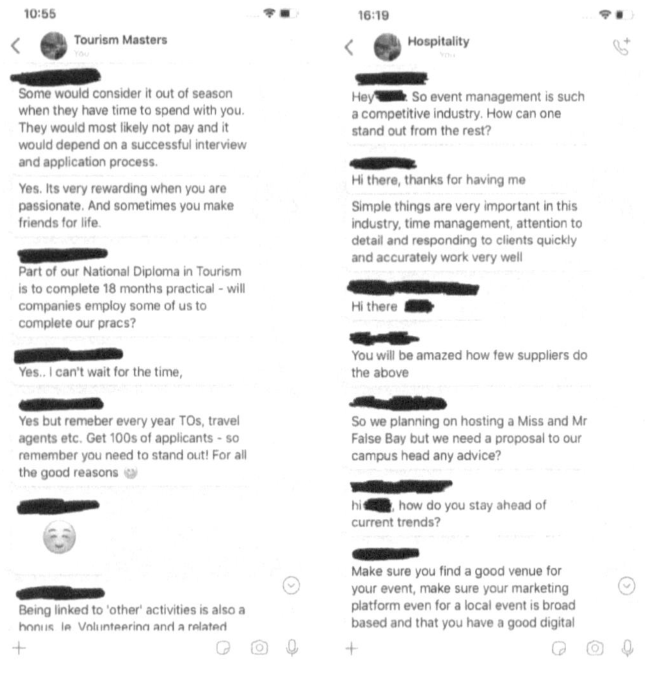


*Figure 11: High levels of engagement of students during SME chats*

**Table 3: More excerpts from the student chats (from WhatsApp)**

*[W]e are ready, really excited to hear what the Head of the Tour Guides is going to say…oooh I have so many questions for her, I've been looking forward to this chat for a long time, bring it on!*

*I for one am really looking forward to this chat with the events guy, because that's where I see myself one day, I am going to run by own company so this is going to help give me tips which is useful and things I can look out for now*

> *already, maybe he can also give us tips guys for that competition we must*
> *arrange*
>
> *[W]ow, that was so informative! I dunno whether to feel excited or depressed*
> *because now I know that when I finish my studies I must study further to be a*
> *Tour Guide, but it sounds like such a great job. Thanks for arranging that lady*
> *to talk to us*
>
> *Thank you so much, that was really informative…he was great, he knew so*
> *much.*
>
> *Flip, that was next level hey guys! Why are we learning about paper ticketing*
> *then and not the electronic ticketing she spoke about? I'm going to ask Miss*
> *tomorrow in class. She had some great experience, I also want to be like that one*
> *day, with so much experience. Thank you for getting her to chat to us, she was*
> *cool.*

Many students also mentioned that the anonymity afforded by the use of the WhatsApp group in the sessions with the SMEs meant that students who were usually very shy and reserved in class, and who regularly did not participate in classroom discussions were more animated and engaged during these online chats.

> *And also, because we didn't actually see them, people who were sometimes shy or*
> *who didn't speak in class, would ask questions in the chat, I don't think they*
> *would've done that in person. So that helped them in a way find their own voice. -*
> **P1**

Employers often criticise the relevance of TVET college content curriculum and training. With limited or no access to industry experts, students are unable to connect the theory they learn in class to the real-world application (Papier, 2017). Furthermore, by not being exposed to industry experts, students do not build the necessary networks they may need to access later for work-based placements, internships or to access job opportunities once they graduate. One student shared how an online discussion with an SME translated into a networking opportunity offline. The student attended an information session and recognised the name of one speaker, who had interacted with the class via WhatsApp (see figure 12). The student who had interacted with the official online, approached the official after the information session, introduced herself and the official recognised her name from the chat. The student remarked how the online chat made the offline interaction easier.

During the unstructured interviews with the lecturers, they mentioned that the SME sessions online, had a spillover effect outside the online chats, with students sharing what they discussed with lecturers, and connecting with SMEs at industry events:

*The class was also abuzz after they spoke with the guests. In particular, they've asked that we change the description on the course pamphlet because it's misleading re: tour guides. Many were very upset about the fact that even once they complete their studies, they won't be qualified tour guides. There was also great shock that tour guides earn so little. Thanks for arranging this. I think it helped them a great deal to gain valuable insight into the industry. I tried getting speakers to come and speak to the class but with very little luck. I guess it's because we're all the way out in Muizenberg. This way is easy because they can just sit at their desk or answer the students' questions from wherever they are.* **Lecturer 1**

*Figure 12: Student screenshot*

## 4.4.4 Enables anytime, anywhere learning

Learning is affected by the context within which it occurs. Many students mentioned this in the interviews. They regard their mobile phones and especially the WhatsApp technology as private and for personal use only; none of the students shared their phones with others and rarely showed the content of WhatsApp chats to others. The definition of personal learning environments (PLEs) for the purposes of this study, is the use of mobile technology to produce a personal and portable learning space to suit the learning needs of the students, irrespective of location or context.

An example of this anywhere, anytime affordance of the mobile technology, is this excerpt from one of the student interviews, relating how another student was able to continue participation in the SME chat even while she was travelling elsewhere at the same time:

*It also didn't take up a lot of time, just like during our lunch breaks for 30 or so*

*minutes, and we could use our phones and eat at the same time. Well, we could be*

*anywhere at that time, that was what was so cool, like I remember when we had the*

*one lady, my classmate had to go somewhere and was in a taxi but still taking part*

*in the chat. She would've missed it if the speaker was in class, like physically.* **P2**

For other students, this mobility aspect was critical but for different reasons, namely that they usually struggled to get access to facilities provided by the college, with many stating that aside from access to these computer facilities at college, neither them nor their families owned a computer at home. Only one of the students interviewed lived less than 15 kilometres away from the college campus, so, for the majority of the students, waiting at the campus to access computers was not an option. Students who lived further away from the campus had to consider the availability and safety of public transport. After a particular time, this was neither guaranteed nor safe.

*It also didn't mean that I needed to book time to use the campus computers, that's*

*always a mission to do! (waves arms) It's always full and busy in that computer*

*room, they call it a lab or something like that, but I just know that when they said*

*to us that there was this programme that we had to use for old exam papers, uhm,*

*I can't remember what it was called, a programme, uhm, Black*

*something...(pauses)...man it was such an effort and schlep to get into that computer*

*room to work on it. I don't own my own computer, well no one in my family owns*

*one, so if it's a computer that must be used, I must make a way during my time at*

*campus. That's not always easy. I live very far from college and must worry about*

*public transport late. So I really liked that I basically could just pull out my phone and check out the stuff there on WhatsApp, sometimes even when I was travelling home.* **P4**

Students also regarded the WhatsApp groups as a abbrev in full? (PLE) because of the timing and type of messages shared with them.

*This was so easy and quick. Short messages we could read before college in the morning and on our way home from college. That was so cool.* **P5**

*Well it was a very different way to use WhatsApp, and I liked some of the methods used. I really enjoyed it because it was easy and I didn't have to learn a new system, it was also simple; on my phone and not inconvenient. I could carry it everywhere and look at the notes all the time and whenever I wanted to, at night or sometimes I'd read stuff when I was travelling.* **P7**

*I also really, really like the way it was done - every morning we got a motivational message, then some stuff we did the day before, then sometime that week we spoke to someone who was doing stuff we were still studying about, like the Gary; the guy from More2Xplore. And then we also had competitions and closer to exams, we revised exam papers and stuff. I would structure my time accordingly to the messages. Like for revision in the afternoons, I made sure that I played background music to block out noise while revising the work. Before the expert chats, I always prepared questions and even used [it] to check out the speakers on Google so I knew a bit about them.* **P2**

### *4.4.5 Provides access to relevant content*

Another prominent theme that emerged from the interviews and observations was access to relevant content. Students responded positively to revision content, industry news, exam tips, and study techniques. The college does provide students with access to Blackboard, a learning management system.  In the pre-study survey to determine student use of their mobiles for learning, less than 5% of students indicated the use of the system. In observations of the groups, students would show appreciation or acknowledgement of the post via responses or emojis. Students would also post questions or requests for more detailed explanations of curriculum content. Figure 13 below shows a selection of screenshots indicating student engagement when content was posted in the groups.

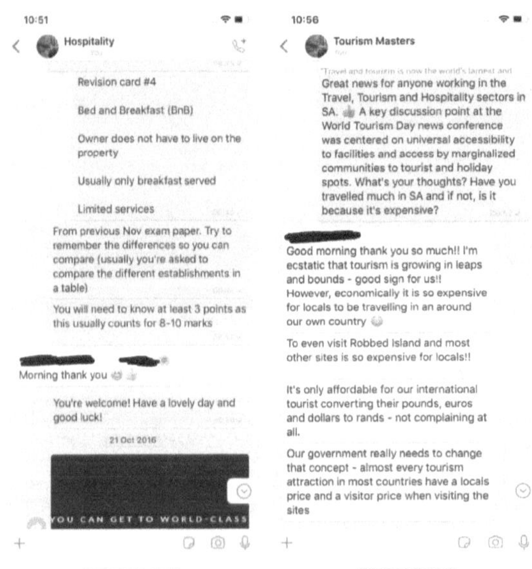


*Figure 13: Screenshots indicating student engagement and reaction to content*

This positive sentiment was supported in the interviews. Students shared how the content posted in the WhatsApp groups helped them revise or keep them abreast of the work covered in the class that day. Some students remarked on the fun way the content was packaged, i.e. quizzes or challenges.

> *I learnt so much…it helped me, no - forced me to revise. I don't think I would've revised on my own if I had to, this worked well for a lazy person like me. You know it surprised me, it's funny how some of the stuff we chatted about in the group helped me revise. I remembered this one screen in exams. Ja! That was funny and cool, because I didn't go over some of the stuff again when I had to study for exams because we got reminders in the group. So, when I saw it in the paper I started to stress but then remembered seeing it on my phone! Very cool for me.* **P5**

> *Like, maybe I didn't go to college. I'd use the group and see what happened that day. I wouldn't then miss out that much because, like my ex-classmates, would post everything in the WhatsApp group, so I'd see what's going on. Then the facilitator would also send short notes to revise the next morning. It helped me a lot.* **P6**

> *I didn't know what to expect when we started, I just knew we were invited to participate, and it sounded cool and like it could help me with my coursework.-* **P1**

> *I was so impressed because, ja (yes) it was about your (college) work but like*

> *in a different way, also fun, with stuff like quizzes.* **P4**

> *It was a different way to learn for us, but everything was useful. It was more than I expected. I like that it didn't feel like work.* **P1**

> *[A]nd posts about our industry or from a newspaper but linked to our industry – very interesting and useful stuff that we definitely didn't get in class.* **P2**

*I did learn more about stuff like in our industry that we didn't learn in class, like about travelling overseas and the tourism stuff and news – it like opened my eyes so much to what is possible in this space.* **P4**

### *4.4.6 Provides motivation and support*

The majority of the students who participated in the study were between the ages of 18-22 years old, and as noted in Chapter 2, this age group, known as the Emerging Adult phase, is typically a challenging period for young people as they straddle adolescence and adulthood. Emerging adults struggle with anxiety, feelings of inadequacy, and have a strong desire to belong to a social unit to feel supported and valued. As noted in Chapter 3, students received inspirational posts every day, which were either hero stories or a motivational quote and image (see Section 3.7).

In the interviews, students reported that these daily inspirational posts, known as "Daily Kickstart" created a stimulating environment. They were spurred on to improve their results and motivated to achieve their long-term career goals. The five-month observation period also witnessed high levels of student motivation. Students would always remark on or react to an inspirational post. Motivated students are likely to be more engaged, and for many of these students, as noted in the pre-study survey, they received little to no familial support for their studies.

*The daily inspirational messages made such a difference in our lives, especially mine; like I remember that there was one day there was no motivational post and we asked, 'where are you' and 'where was our message'? Because, like I was so down because I failed and they just put me over and I had to re-write one subject and I really wanted to give up then and then this group came along at just the right time, it motivated me with those messages; it gave me that boost I needed. I used to write it down and asked my mommy to type it and print it for me on little cards that I've posted on my wall. I still look at them for support.* **P7**

*Also, the inspirational stuff, sho. It, like, helped me believe in myself so much. I don't have family or people pushing me, and that was nice. I kept some of the stuff. It was so nice to have this sent every day. Except, (laughs), there was one day where there was no post and everyone in the class asked if it was being stopped and I wrote and asked and I was relieved to hear it wasn't. - P3*

*[T]he positive stuff just helped start the day correctly. We definitely felt in a better mood, okay, me, I did!* **P6**

*[B]ut we also got inspirational messages, so it felt like there was always a positive space to go to, where I didn't feel silly to ask questions or make mistakes and who sent me positive message and fist bumps before tests and exams, we even did revision together. Eish, I can go on! It was just so, so nice!* **P5**

*During the exams, I was, like, feeling so down and then boom! A message appeared, like a motivational message for the class, and the words just meant something, like, deep to me...(pause )Ja, it meant a lot to me at that exact moment and made me believe I could pass and more than that, that I could become someone, do something big with my life. Every day after that I really looked forward to seeing what we'd get that day for the message. It made me work harder that exams.* **P4**

When the researcher probed further as to why the P4 student did not seek further assistance from a counsellor at college, this is the response given:

*The college had this guy who was available for issues like that but, he always looked scattered. Shame, it's like he also needed to talk to someone. He seemed super busy all the time, always helping new students with stuff, so I just didn't bother. Besides, in this*

The screenshots below (figure 14) are illustrative of the types of student interaction/reaction to the motivational posts. The students' names have been blacked out and appear on the left (white background), with the researcher/facilitator on the right (green background):

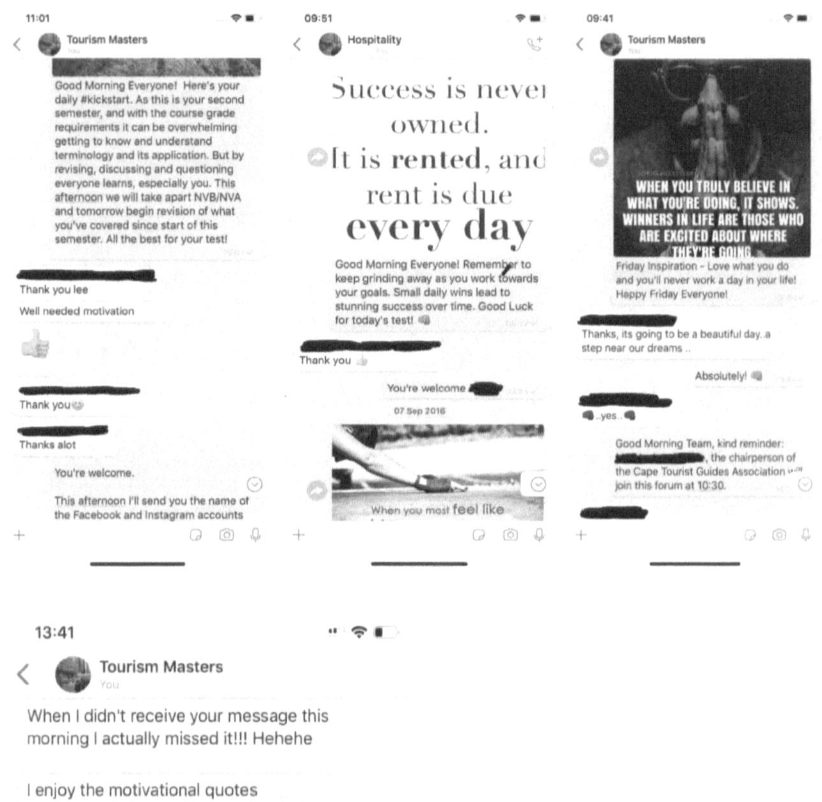

*Figure 14: Types of student interaction and reaction to the motivational posts*

Aside from feeling motivated, students also felt that the WhatsApp chats made them feel supported and heard, crucial during the Emerging Adult phase, and also an area in TVETs that is critically under-resourced (Van Breda, 2017). Students expressed feelings of frustration and despair regarding their studies and the quality of their qualifications. Anxiety around securing meaningful employment post-college dominated was another dominant theme during these interactions. Students felt that the groups were a safe space to vent and share with the facilitator and their peers. The next two screenshots (figure 15) from the WhatsApp group illustrate the freedom student felt in being able to share their concerns and vent their frustrations in the groups.

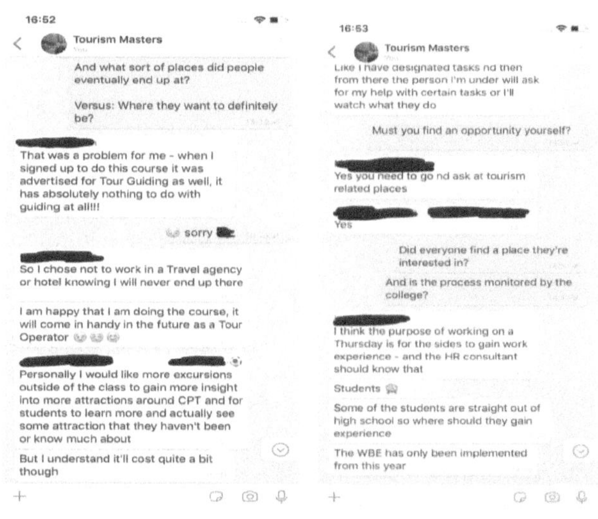


*Figure 15: Student posts sharing their feelings regarding aspects of college*

### 4.4.7 Social Learning

Chapter 2 explored social learning as a possible learning theory that can suit mlearning contexts. Social learning theory asserts that the understanding of a subject increases when there is meaningful interaction between people. Interviewees described their experience of using WhatsApp to communicate with other students and the facilitator about their course. Many mentioned the learning benefits derived from being part of such a group and said that this virtual community became a safe space to learn. The virtual community aspect was also evident in observations, students would assist one another with coursework, and would also share their work-based experiences with their peers via their WhatsApp group chats (figure 16 and figure 17).

*It made me feel like I wasn't stupid, and no question was stupid, the facilitator person always said that, and it was something I remember even now, like I speak up at work and I'm not shy to ask any question.* **P4**

*Yes definitely, in that group we learnt not to be shy and answer stuff and ask stuff that sometimes we didn't know, like you didn't feel embarrassed that you didn't know, you grew from that and learnt from others, we all learned together and laughed together (laughs).* **P6**

*Well, like I said before it was a great experience, it really changed how I think about stuff and my own studies. I liked being part of it and was sad when it finished. And that we didn't have something the next year like that, it was informative, like educational, I learnt so much and not just about my course, other things about tourism; but it was also great that I could connect with my class and we discussed stuff we were all struggling with, and they helped me sometimes, and so did the facilitator. Knowing there was a group that I could quickly turn to when I needed help about the course made me feel safe, I didn't stress about stuff I didn't understand immediately in class, if I didn't 'get it' in class, I'd take it to the group later. Plus, I could ask stuff at any time, that was convenient. Like say I remembered a question I had about ticketing, and remembered at 8 at night, I could send the question then and get help from everyone. It was like a google but just for my class.* **P7**

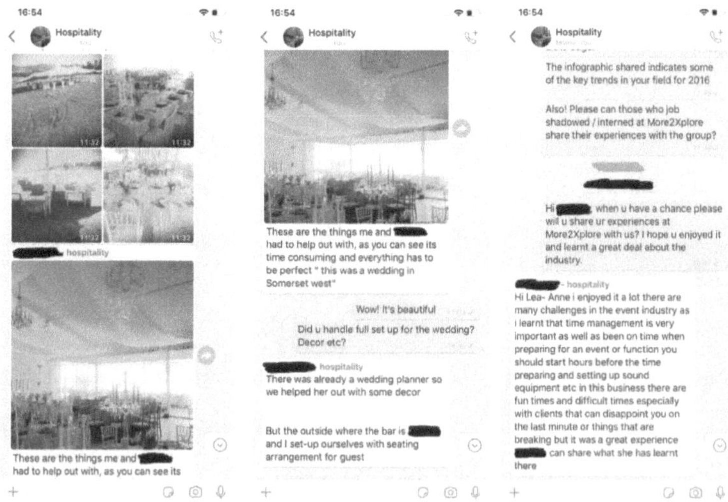

*Figure 16: Peer to Peer learning*

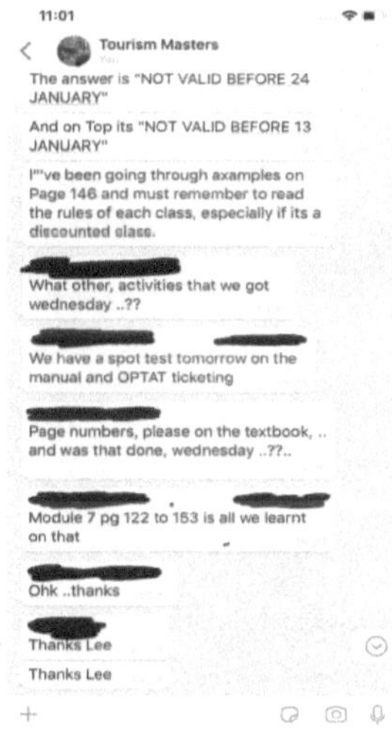

*Figure 17: Student discussion pre-test*

Interestingly, during the student interviews, almost all the students mentioned how the WhatsApp group encouraged students to participate in discussions on the group whose native language was not English. These students ordinarily did not participate in discussions in their classroom.

*[T]here were some students who in class were shy I think because English wasn't maybe their mother language but, on the group,, they all said something. It was nice to hear from them for a change.* **P2**

*It was great. Because my class was made up of a lot of people who came from townships and they didn't speak much in the class. They were very quiet. I don't know if it was because they didn't speak English well, but somma all of a sudden, on the group, they were chatting. That was nice. I liked hearing from them and sometimes when I agreed with what they were saying I used to send an emoji, and next time in class I used to use it as a reason to chat to them.* **P4**

One of the lecturers echoed this sentiment, as they noticed a difference in the class, with the students whose mother tongue was not English, who had previously been very hesitant to speak in class, now participated more freely, and the class as whole were a more cohesive unit, supportive of one another in the classroom. This lecturer had initially indicated that they thought the WhatsApp study would not receive much support from the class because of the language issues and the class was quite fractured because of it; this is an excerpt of an interview done before the commencement of the WhatsApp intervention:

*[T]his is the weaker class of the two N4 classes that I teach. I wish you worked with the A group. They're far more engaged and astute...there's also very little engagement or interest shown in the work beyond the classroom, and even there, it's a struggle. I'm also worried that non-English speakers will struggle to understand what's expected of them in a virtual space because that's what happens*

*now already. Then I feel that most of these students still act as if they're at school. There's no ownership of the work or their role in the class or interest even in what they're learning outside this class. I'm struggling to connect with the non-English students, they never say anything in the class.* **Lecturer 1**

The participation of students in the WhatsApp groups helped to foster a learning community online, as well as offline, which did not exist before the study. They also interacted more socially with each other offline. This online community of practice has prevailed. Some of the students created their own WhatsApp group after this research study ended. They use the newly formed group to connect with their classmates, share the learning from their internships, as well as provide a supportive community.

*I got more closer to my classmates. Like before, we were all doing our own thing and then we became more closer, you understand. Before everyone was doing their own thing, everyone was like "hi, hi, hi" then through this WhatsApp group we got to know each other more, you understand, ja. Before this class WhatsApp group. we didn't really have a class chat group. We started it at the beginning of the year. Like before this one that you created, but everything fell apart within two weeks because everyone was sending all this stupid stuff and then you came and then I started to get a lot from that like for my work.* **P6**

*What I would like to say is that WhatsApp group brought us together because we all like were all over the place, but it brought us together, and it also taught me that you need other people, you need to lean on other people because like everything was being shared in that group, you understand? Like some things I never understood before, but it was just explained in that group so nicely. So you know it's nice that it did that because like even now, people in my class that were in that group, we still communicate with each*

### 4.4.8 Incentivises learning

The WhatsApp intervention also invoked healthy competition amongst students, via the challenges. These challenges tested students' knowledge of their curriculum; and designed to test how they applied curriculum content in real-world situations. Initially, the clues of the challenges were posted on social media, a dedicated Facebook and Instagram page, but after requests from students, copied and shared in the WhatsApp groups. Initially, students paired up to work in teams; the next round of challenges was for individuals only. The challenge winners received various prizes - ranging from shopping vouchers to experiences linked to their studies. These experiential prizes provided students with opportunities to learn about their field of study. One prize, tickets onboard a popular tourist 'hop-on/hop-off' bus enabled Travel and Tourism student to experience the city through the lens of a tourist. Other popular prizes included mobile data and airtime.

*The class was hyper during challenge time because everyone was talking about*

*their college work. It was great to see them all so excited about their studies!*

*Generally, the whole class seemed in better spirits throughout this first batch of*

*messages, especially the challenge, and of course the prizes were a big drawcard.*

**Lecturer 2**

*I used to ask a lot of questions about the work but also about the challenges we were*

*set. That was like so cool! I really enjoyed that a lot.* **P5**

*I used to brag about it a lot. The questions you asked in the challenges made me*

*like interested in the other cultures, in life outside of our classroom. Like when*

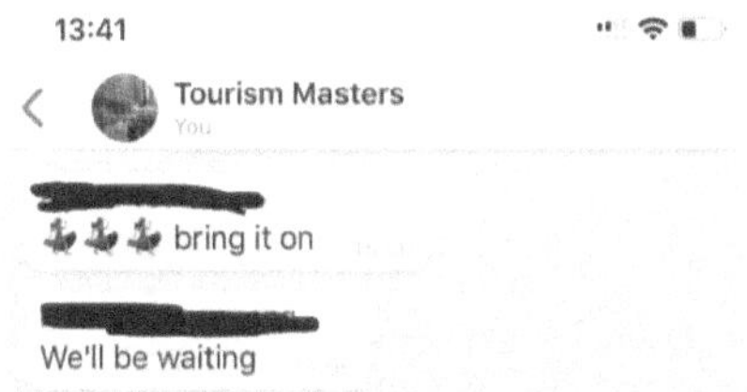



*Figure 18: Student enthusiasm pre-challenge*

Challenge content remained popular throughout the study. Students would post many questions related to the challenges. It was interesting to note that in one class (Travel and Tourism) interest in the challenges decreased after one student won back-to-back challenges but increased again after a different student won the next challenge.

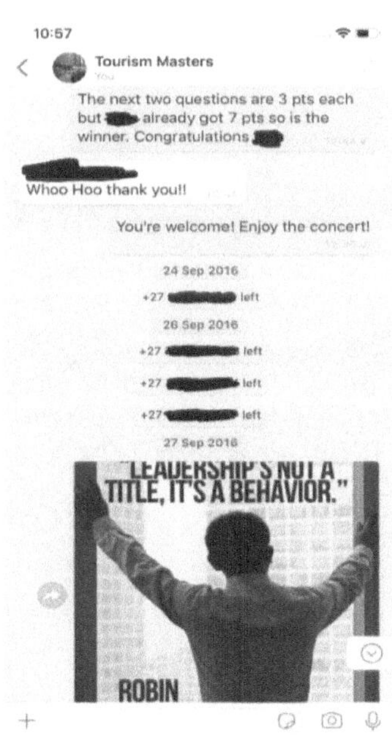



*Figure 19: Students left the WhatsApp group after one student won two weeks in a row*

**4.5 Factors that inhibit the successful use of mtech by students**

The two main factors that emerged from the data that best explains what inhibited the successful use of mtech by students were data costs and college pressures and time.

*4.5.1 Data costs*

All the students interviewed indicated that they had Cell C mobile phones subscriber Identification Model (SIM) cards. The students in this study regarded Cell C as the cheapest mobile network in the country. It was, therefore, a favourite and preferred network amongst students primarily because of its affordable data packages, and the zero-rated WhatsApp (that it had at one stage). One student referenced the affordability in her interview when asked to describe what it was like to use WhatsApp to communicate with other students and the facilitator about her course. Here is what she said:

> *It was very nice. Like WhatsApp is very cheap as well, like you can buy data for R12 for a whole month and use it for a whole month on Cell C but you can only use it on WhatsApp. You don't use for other social networks; you can only do it for WhatsApp. It lasts like the whole month. Like with WhatsApp you can also do a voice note.* **P6.**

Another student also explicitly referenced the affordability of WhatsApp on the Cell C network in his interview:

> *It didn't cost me anything and I think a lot of [other] people [too] because most of my class used Cell C so WhatsApp was free.* **P5.**

Students received the challenges via the two WhatsApp groups. They then had to use Instagram and Facebook to search for clues linked to the challenges. The pre-study survey indicated that these two social media platforms were popular amongst the students. However, after the initial engagement on Instagram (for the first challenge), students asked the facilitator to create a Facebook group and post the clues there. Later, they requested that all challenge clues only be posted in the WhatsApp groups. Use of these platforms required data, and the relatively cheap Cell C packages excluded social media use other than WhatsApp. The following interview excerpt illustrates student frustrations regarding data cost issues:

*A big issue for our class was when the challenge clues were posted on Facebook. This would eat into our data big time! So we just avoided it and we were sad and upset because the prizes for the challenges were always so cool and we wanted to be able to at least see the clues so we could give it our best shot to win the prize. So I remember for the first challenge we just kept quiet about it and didn't participate, but I think that because only like two people in the whole class joined the page, the facilitator asked if there was an issue and then we said something about the data.* **P2.**

*We all tried to work hard to win the stuff because there was always cool prizes, and like there you even made exceptions, because you also put stuff, uhm, the clues, neh? on Instagram and Facebook and that uses a lot of data but then when we complained you posted the same stuff on our group. You even allowed us to send you the answers outside of the group but still on WhatsApp so the others couldn't see our answers instead of mailing it, because that wasn't always so easy, and again, uses data.* **P5.**

*A drawback for me would be that on some of the quiz stuff we needed to look at the Facebook and Instagram posts and those used a lot of data, but even then we worked around it - one of us would use data to look at it and screenshot it and send to us on WhatsApp, and later the group coordinator also sent it on WhatsApp so all the clues were there where we could find it.* **P7.**

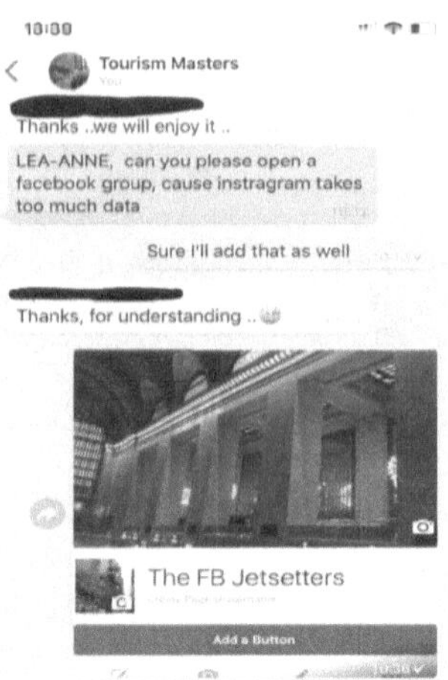


*Figure 20: Student request for Facebook group creation*

### 4.5.2 College pressures and time

Other factors inhibiting students' successful use of mtech include time and college workload pressures. Earlier, in section 4.4.4 students listed convenience, i.e. the 'anytime, anywhere' affordance presented by the WhatsApp group as being a contributory factor for their successful use of the groups. However, four of the seven students interviewed indicated that they could have derived even more benefit from the WhatsApp group if they did not always feel under pressure in class and college. It was interesting that all four of these students were N5 students. They (N5 students) have more stringent deadlines to meet in terms of Work-Based Experience journals, in preparation for the N6 year. The college expects that after successful completion of N5, students spend 18 months as an intern in their field of study. The result is that most N5 students spend a large proportion of their time researching and reaching out to organisations to secure a suitable internship.

The N5 Travel and Tourism students' timetable also seemed to change more frequently than the N4 Hospitality students, leading to uncertainty amongst students. Sudden changes in the class timetable meant rescheduling SME chats. Many students in the groups expressed anger and frustration at the unforeseen change to their timetables. Students used the following words, phrases and questions between 9-11 times each throughout observation to convey their annoyance and frustration at the time table changes: "annoyed", "how do they expect us to learn like this?", "they never stick to plans." The eye-rolling emoticon featured 20 times while the use of the 'see no evil' emoticon featured 15 times directly following an abrupt change to their timetable resulting in an SME chat being rescheduled. The use of the emoticons conveyed the students' frustration at the change of plans by the lecturers.

This unpredictability then sometimes affected the planning that students did prior to these expert chats. Below are interview excerpts that describe this frustration:

*I liked this group and I feel like I did benefit a lot from it but maybe I could've benefited more. I just felt that sometimes our chats were rushed or moved because of college work and that really wasn't fair to us. We looked forward especially to when there were experts, because most of us were preparing for our internship period and wanted to understand what these people from the industry expected from us. So, we couldn't always prepare well for these chats.* **P4**

*One time the class was really looking forward to chatting with this one lady who worked in corporate travel. Her background was very interesting because she had worked on cruise liners and many of us wanted to work on a ship. So, we made arrangements to sit together at lunch so we could plan how we were going to tackle the chat to get the most out of it, but then our lecturer told us just before the break that we had to stay in to complete forms that the college needed from us. So, we had to let the facilitator know just then, and the guest. That was embarrassing but I was also very upset because when we set up a time again to chat to her, I couldn't be on the chat, so I missed out.* **P6**

The N5 students interviewed also indicated that their college workloads were incredibly high, which sometimes meant they did not respond on chats when questions or revision notes were posted. In observing the groups, it was evident when the students were very busy with college work, as the engagement was generally high. During highly stressful times, the engagement level would drop, or someone would post to say everyone is probably studying or completing a college assignment due the next day, or they would post emoticons that showed a book or a smiley face with spectacles, to indicate they were studying.

> *It's not that we didn't want to chat, but you must understand that in N5 it was hectic. Sjoe, we had so much work to do, it was just crazy! I would see the messages come up and wanted to read but didn't have time because I was busy with my college work.* **P2**

> *During exams I found the group chats a little irritating because like I was trying to be calm and revise and then someone would ask a question before an exam, like, 'explain this or explain that' and then if I couldn't remember it, I'd panic and start stressing and then want to go through my work again. So that wasn't great for me. Then I was gonna mute the chat but got worried I'd miss out on something important.* **P7**

> *The group chats where people were revising didn't help me because some people - eish, just didn't understand their work, and I think didn't maybe also, like **actually** study and were using the group for that. There was one time when someone was asking questions and it was so obvious this person didn't understand their work and they kept asking people to help them understand it, like the day before the exam. I mean! (rolls eyes) So yes those chats didn't help me. Like I think maybe before a test the group must keep quiet so that people can study in peace and not hear 'ping' 'ping' 'cause then you check your phone.* **P5**

Owing to college pressures and sudden changes to timetables, students offered suggestions for improvements that could support the successful student use of the WhatsApp group. The screenshot below is part of one suggestion. The writer requested that the class receive messages in the morning and afternoon, during the time they would ordinarily commute.

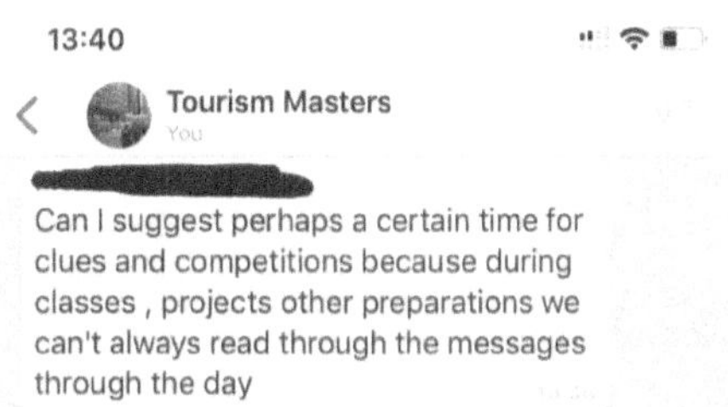


*Figure 21: Student suggestion for specific times for posting of challenges and content*

## 4.6 Recommendations to Support Student Use of mtech

To address this question about what could further support the successful use of mtech so that learning can be enhanced, the data was clear: greater integration within the broader college experience and specifically, with their courses. The students interviewed all overwhelmingly stated that their overall experience of the use of mtech was positive but, they also noted that it should have been extended and used by other students at the college and that lecturers should use it as a tool to supplement the in-classroom lectures.

*Just it was a great experience, I know my college was testing it at the time, and like I will say they must continue with this. It's also better than using an app, because the data wasn't hectic, and it must be driven by someone who's not a student. It was fun and cool because it never felt like 'Oh my gosh, now I must do this' it was just like a chat that you were part of, even if you didn't say anything, you were always learning. I think that it had to be extended and not just for like the course, like why don't they somma register you on it when you start college? There's so many things you need assistance with when you start studying at college. It's so confusing and sometimes overwhelming that having this on your phone helps and you can ask a question at any time about your studies and like career stuff will really help people. Like, I liked it for our course, but it will be of even more help if people use it from the time they start college. Even now, we don't get enough college help for our studies and career. And now this is over, and you're back to struggling on your own to find answers.* **P3**

*Overall I really liked using this and being part of the group. It made a big impact on my life. I learned some stuff that I still use now. It was just a little sad that like those in my class who were on the chat, were closer and the others not part of the group seemed left out. But also, our lecturer didn't even try to use some of the methods that were used in the group, in his lectures. Like the challenge and quiz stuff was so much fun. We had to apply the theory stuff in a practical way to solve clues. He should've done the same in class. It would've made it so much more interesting sitting in that class.* **P5**

Two students also specifically referenced the college years that they felt would have made the best use of the groups :

*I just feel that this should be used not only in N4 and for one course, but all courses man, we would've benefited more. Like now we're all doing internships and there's no group for us as a class, so it would've been cool to be in one now, getting tips and advice or even just keeping in touch and hearing what other people were experiencing.* **P1**

*Just, like, can I make a suggestion? I think it was very cool to have the experts and stuff but I think it was wasted on us in N4. Like the N6-ers would've benefited more. Do you know what I mean?* **P6**

P6 explains further:

*Well. like the N6-ers are almost finished with their studies and like getting ready to go work so they would've made even better use of the experts' time. Not that we wasted it but just they would've been able to ask for jobs and stuff. For us that stuff was still a far way away but not for them or for me now. So ja, maybe you should do it with N6-ers They'll really appreciate it. (laughs) Like now I study N6, so it would've helped me a lot.*
**P6**

Other students listed that they would have appreciated unrestricted access to the assistance offered on the WhatsApp groups (the facilitator did not communicate after 8 pm or before 7 am), greater personalisation so that it was better suited to their particular needs.

*I think that maybe also it would've been nice to have it available at all times, like a college and career Google so you can ask other questions that maybe wasn't linked to only your course. Stuff like exams and more career kind of stuff and exam prep stuff. I sometimes felt too shy to ask it in the group.* **P2**

*Listen don't get me wrong, I really enjoyed this WhatsApp group and I learned a lot from it and enjoyed all the chats, but I think if the college wants to roll it out, then they must also maybe think of something that's like just for me to chat with, like you know, like a personal coach or something. Because I did like have some stress around my exams and especially about finding an internship, and I didn't always want to put it out there on the chat because then some people may think*

*I'm an idiot and I just don't want everyone knowing my business. I also had some issues with my fees, and it's always a mission to sort that at the fees office at college, always long lines and embarrassing because everyone can see you standing there. I would've liked to be able to ask those questions to the college or someone who knows those answers and get a reply, but not in the group. Like the group worked well for other stuff. That made learning fun, and I appreciate that, but like the personal and admin stuff, that would be nice to ask outside the group and chat about without feeling exposed. I dunno if that's possible still on WhatsApp, or if it's like expensive, but yes as a recommendation for improving, that's what I would add, but you mustn't get rid of the groups, because like I said I did learn and it was fun to get to know my classmates in that way, but this will just like take this to the next level. Also, it mustn't be like a separate app, because then we must use data to use it, where this was easy for everyone to use because it was on WhatsApp, so like we were used to it, and it always felt just like a chat, nothing I had to figure out.* **P5**

## 4.7 Chapter Conclusion

This chapter presented the findings of the research. Included in the findings, is an explanation of the analysis used to determine the themes which answer the research sub-questions. Given the ubiquity of mobile phones, it is hard to believe that it was almost fifty years ago that Martin Cooper, an engineer at Motorola, made the world's first mobile phone call from a handset that weighed an astonishing 1,1kg. Today, the average mobile phone weighs between 150g-200g and represents far more than merely an instrument to speak to another person; thanks to advances in its technology, it now allows people to transact, share photos, film, play music, look up information and so much more. Undoubtedly, mobile phones have made our lives easier, because it has made these services more accessible. A common thread across all themes was that of accessibility – of the technology itself, as well as what the technology gives the user access to – in the case of the study this included access to subject matter experts, incentives, psychosocial support, and industry information.

Given the socio-economic context in which the study takes place, it is important to remember that most students hail from impoverished communities and households, and their access to technology is limited to their mobile phones. Most mobile learning programmes and projects that seek to address problems in the educational sector through the use of technology, usually embark on a quest to develop a technology tool that's novel, and while it may offer solutions, it can also be problematic.

In this study, there was no need to overcome these technology accessibility barriers because there was no need for the students first to learn how to use the technology (hardware and software). The hardware was already familiar to the students because it was their mobile phone. In this study, WhatsApp was used, as it was familiar to all the students. None of the students needed to download it, as they all already used it and none required assistance with using it. The researcher also did not have to explain any cyber etiquette to the students for group engagement. Students like interview participant P2 noted this familiarity with the WhatsApp technology: "And it was cool to use something that was simple. No one had to teach us how to use WhatsApp, I mean, come on, who doesn't know how to use WhatsApp?" It is evident then from this statement that the students felt comfortable using WhatsApp technology.

Introducing and rolling out an mlearning programme in an educational setting is fraught with angst, despite the opportunities it may hold. People are hesitant to sign up if they think it will not be straightforward to participate because most times, using and engaging technology means they first need to master the use of the hardware and software. Accessibility to the external experts, psychosocial support (in the form of daily motivational messages).

Students also regarded the technology as an enabler. Access to external experts and support is limited to what the college offers – and as the study's findings show, this was either non-existent or stretched.  Student P4 mentioned in their interview that while the college provided access to a counsellor, they did not utilise the services offered because they felt that his (the counsellor's) schedule seemed stressful and feared rejection because of this.

However, with this WhatsApp group, the technology-facilitated access to support, via daily motivational messages. This support mattered a great deal to the students who like P7 utilised it outside of the group. P7 shared that they had failed and had been promoted by the college. This student indicated how this action left them feeling shameful and depressed. However, for them, the motivational posts arrived soon afterwards and helped them to feel better about themselves and their own achievements. The student shared these posts with a parent and asked that the parent type it and print it so that it could be posted on the walls in their bedroom as sources of motivation.

Access to external experts was almost non-existent at the college, but something that was made possible via the WhatsApp group, and students like P1 appreciated it. They shared that what they found most useful was the caliber of experts that they interacted with in the chats. They were especially appreciative of the advice and guidance that these experts shared, which the students did not received in the classroom.

Industry expert engagements like these allowed students to access job opportunities later and build industry networks. Students recognised the power that mobile technology afforded them. Their mobile phones provided them with access (via the WhatsApp groups) to content and services that could potentially improve their lives. However, exorbitant data costs thwarted their desire and curtailed efforts. Students listed the high cost of data as the primary reason they did not access the Facebook and Instagram channels during the challenges. As we move further along in this networked society, governments and educational institutions must enable access to connectivity – either at a reduced fee or legislate that mobile network operators zero-rate their platforms for educational purposes. It appears that only if this is enabled, can the full potential of mlearning become unlocked. In Chapter 5, this will be explored further, along with a discussion of the study's findings, the implications thereof, the limitations of the study and suggestions for further research.

# CHAPTER 5: RESEARCH CONCLUSIONS

## 5.1. Introduction

For Generation Z, who grew up with the internet, and in an ever-present flicker of either a computer or mobile phone screen, technology is an integral part of their lives. Thus, using technology to learn is not a jarring prospect for them. The purpose of this qualitative case study is to explore the experiences of students using mobile technology for their learning. It did not, however, form part of their formal curriculum, and they made use of it outside the classroom.

The premise of the study is that students who have a good mlearning experience relate that to the institutional learning experience. If students feel supported, valued and have a clear understanding of how their studies fit into the broader industry, they will feel hopeful about their future and motivated to work hard and complete their studies. If students feel motivated to work harder, it may lead to an increase in the number of students completing their studies and graduating. As more students graduate, the throughput rates at TVET colleges will improve, and hopefully this will lead to the increased employment of young people.

Today, there is a great focus on 4IR technologies globally. In South Africa, the former education minister appointed a commission to explore the impact of 4IR technologies and advise of the steps needed to prepare young people adequately for a 4IR workplace (Kahn, 2019). College leaders should, therefore, consider the possible applications of technology that already reside within their institutions and that students already use.

Despite South Africa regarding itself as a 'mobile-first' nation, there is very little research that focuses on mlearning in higher education and training institutions. The majority of the research in this area centres on universities. The literature supports this; however, only one case study has focused on TVET colleges. This chapter presents a summary of the current study, its limitations and the conclusions drawn from the findings, and concludes with suggestions for future research.

## 5.2 Overview of the Study

Over the last two decades, South Africa has seen a proliferation of mlearning projects and programmes. At the same time, mobile phone ownership and usage in the country experienced explosive growth and is now almost ubiquitous. It is surprising, therefore, that very little research has been focused on the mlearning experience of students. Most studies have focused on the quantitative outputs of students using mlearning programmes; namely, has the mlearning intervention resulted in an improvement in their performance in an academic subject? Where the focus has been on students' emotions regarding mlearning interventions, none of these studies are located within the context of a TVET college. International organisations, such as UNEVOC, and locally, at the conference of the South African Chapter of the International Vocational Educational Training Association (IVETA) the focus of most of the discussions was on the benefits afforded by technology, including mobile devices in the TVET college space.

False Bay College provides all its students with access to e-learning resources via Blackboard, a learner management system (LMS). The portal, called 'My FBC', is provided at no cost to the student but great expense to the college. However, as noted earlier in the study, student uptake of the portal is minimal. Given the increased focus on the use of technology to enhance student learning within education in South Africa and the disconnect at colleges between technology supplied and technology used by students, it is clear that the leadership at the TVETs critically needs to engage with and understand the advantages of mobile technology. Leaders have to understand it primarily from the perspective of their students so that they can provide learner-centred education, a key component of Target 4.7[1] of the Sustainable Development Goals of (UNESCO, 2017).

It is hoped, therefore, that through this study's exploration of student experiences using their mobile phones for learning, educational leaders will be better equipped to make decisions regarding the use and implementation of mobile technology in their institutions. The literature supports this call to focus on the learning experience of students using mobile technology rather than on the technology itself (Traxler, 2016).

The study's main question is: How can mobile technology enhance students' learning experiences in technical vocational training in South Africa? In order to fully explore this

---

[1] Target 4.7. By 2030, ensure that all learners acquire knowledge and skills needed to promote sustainable development, including, among others, through education for sustainable development and sustainable lifestyles, human rights, gender equality, promotion of a culture of peace and nonviolence, global citizenship and appreciation of cultural diversity and of culture's contribution to sustainable development. Source: United Nations, 2015

open-ended question, the following research sub-questions were answered: What contributory factors led to the students' successful use of the mtech? What factors inhibit students' use of the mtech? What changes would students want that would support the use of tech for learning? As this is an exploratory study focused on a real-life setting, i.e. a TVET college, a qualitative case study is used to answer the study's research questions.

The exploratory aspect seeks to answer an open-ended 'how' question, the research methodology employed strategy, data collection techniques, and analysis that would allow the students' voices and perspectives to emerge. For this reason, a qualitative study design was used (Stake, 2010). It guaranteed the capture of the authentic student mlearning experience. A case study approach is used, focusing on the single-bounded case of False Bay College, drawing on multiple sources of data collection (unstructured and semi-structured interviews, as well as observations of the students in the WhatsApp groups) These data collection methods enable the researcher to gain an in-depth understanding of how students at a TVET college experienced an mlearning intervention, and the study gains insight into which aspects of the intervention worked well, and which did not work well, as well as the recommendations for the implementation of such an intervention.

The findings resolve the research question. Overall, the students' experience of mlearning is positive and regarded as successful. Such a positive experience is encouraging for college leadership at this particular institution. It is also encouraging for other educational leaders who are contemplating the use of mobile technology at their respective institutions. The study shows that a fresh approach for how learning is viewed, coupled with the use of simple, ubiquitous technology, that is already in the hands of students, is a logical way forward.

## 5.3 Conclusions and Implications

*5.3.1 Mlearning encourages peer to peer learning, creates Communities of Practice and fosters cultural and language inclusivity*

All students interviewed stated that they enjoyed using WhatsApp to connect and learn from their peers and SMEs. Similarly, the researcher also observed this enthusiastic exchange between students using the WhatsApp group. Daily, there was high engagement amongst students: they would either be explaining concepts and posting questions to their classmates, the facilitator or SME or debating a trending topic. They would also share photographs of experiences and would acknowledge others' input (including the facilitator) with emojis or symbols. Students remarked on the special collegial relationship that existed between students on the WhatsApp group, that did not exist offline.

The literature supports this finding where researchers found that one of the contributory success factors of the Mo Maths programme was its peer-supported learning. Similar to this study, the high school learners, who were enrolled in the programme to improve their maths marks, also connected and learned from each other and the facilitator via the chat platform, using their mobile phones. Other researchers state that even if a student does not participate in an activity (e.g. conversation), they are still learning by participating (observing/reading) from the side-line. Similarly, in this study, not all students participated in the WhatsApp group discussions or reacted to posts. However, they derived value from being in the group – reading messages, observing interactions (words, symbols and sometimes emoji responses).

Students comment in the study about how much they enjoyed interacting with their peers in the WhatsApp groups. Throughout this research, the students checked in daily to the WhatsApp group to share content and ideas and to ask for assistance. From the literature, these are all characteristics of a Community of Practice (CoP), i.e.a group who work together and bond either because of a shared passion or interest. More than just being a descriptor, membership of CoPs has distinct advantages. It encourages critical thinking, improves students 'problem-solving', communication and collaboration skills. This was shown in the findings of this study. Students shared how the groups made them feel supported in a safe environment where they were allowed to ask questions, unafraid that it could be deemed as a stupid or silly question.

Furthermore, from the observations of the groups, it was noted how even when engaged in intense debate, the students still respected and trusted one another always to resolve issues amicably. In the literature, Brown (2003) supports the use of CoPs for learning, stating that the 'community mind' that emerges from these engagements not only makes effective use of existing resources but also helps students improve their communication and analytical skills. It helps them engage more deeply with the content, and also encourages them to contribute to the pool of knowledge. CoPs afford Gen Z with the opportunity to co-create their learning experience and fosters inclusion, imperative for their buy-in.

An interesting and unexpected finding of the study was hearing from the students that the online CoP led to offline social engagement between students. In the one group of students, there was a disconnect between the students in the classroom, but the online experience was different. One of the students shared how the WhatsApp group helped classmates to forge a bond that continued post-study. For them, that was remarkable because they did not initially think that the WhatsApp group would be as beneficial as it turned out to be. It afforded them a space to share their challenges with respect to college work but also to get to know each other better.

In the literature, Dietrich et al. (2014) reference a study where a social media platform was used to encourage extra contact time between students and lecturers. Not only did this virtual increased contact time result in improved academic performance, but it also had an interesting effect – shy students interacted more with lecturers online than they would offline. Similarly, in this study, language differences were a great concern to one of the lecturers. Lecturer 1 was concerned that non-native English speakers would not participate in an online group, just as they did not participate in the classroom. However, this was not the case. Surprisingly, one of the findings of this study was how non-native English speakers, who were reserved and quiet in the classroom, were more active online. The non-native English speakers first started engaging using the emojis or 'mobile phone speak' with their other classmates and later this expanded to engaging with SMEs and the facilitator. Other mainly English native speaking students noticed this and then engaged the non-native English speakers offline, as well.

This finding has important implications for inclusivity and diversity at educational institutions in South Africa, where there are students with diverse cultural backgrounds who speak different languages. Perhaps mlearning can be further explored to see if, through the creation of these virtual CoPs centred around learning, knowledge exchange and collaboration, it can also address issues of inclusivity. The inclusivity offered by virtual COPs may benefit physically challenged students who are unable to attend lectures in person or students who experience exclusion because of ethnicity, gender, or race. However, these factors were not established in the findings, nor were they mentioned in the literature covered, and, therefore, offer an opportunity to be explored in future research.

*5.3.2 Preferring the guide on the (out)side to the sage on the stage*

Students rated the external facilitation of the WhatsApp group very high. They felt it was a contributory factor to the success of the mlearning initiative. Most students had prior experience of using college-linked WhatsApp groups. Some of these college-linked groups were created and managed by their peers. According to the students interviewed, these groups failed because the students who managed the groups were not organised and did not have a coherent plan to host discussions every day.

Furthermore, it did not feel (according to interviewees) like the participating students were intent on using those groups for learning purposes. Many of these student-run groups failed. In the instances where it continued, the groups focused on the social aspects of student life at college. According to lecturers, the WhatsApp groups that they facilitated did not seem to fare any better. Lecturers said they were surprised that a large number of students signed up for the study WhatsApp groups and that a possible reason student did not join the WhatsApp group they created was that it felt like an extension of college, or because the students felt that it was strange to communicate with the lecturer after-hours. The lecturer reported that the primary function of the WhatsApp group they created was to send students extra coursework and test dates.

External facilitation seemed to contribute to a positive experience for students and an overall successful initiative. The literature supports this. In the Namibian case study (Mbukusa, 2018), external facilitators communicated daily with university students to help improve their English comprehension and test scores. All interactions took place in a WhatsApp group. Students rated and reported that they found the groups useful and the exchanges with the external facilitators helpful in improving their English skills. Furthermore, they attributed the positivity they felt about the groups, to the informality of the groups. Moreover, while it is not explicitly stated, the informality could be understood to mean, 'outside the university' domain which external facilitator represented.

Similarly, in this study, the findings show that over the five months, students became more trusting of the external facilitator. This trust was evident in the language they used; it changed from a formal title, for example, "Miss" to the use of first names (informal). In order to build and nurture this trusting environment, students needed to reassurance that their data was protected, and the conversations were confidential. Before the study, these students mainly used WhatsApp to communicate with friends and family. These conversations were mainly for social purposes. In the same way, conversations with lecturers using technology that is owned by them, so deemed a personal space, probably felt jarring, as no aspect of it was social, fun or rewarding, but an extension of the classroom experience (with the same formality).

This finding has implications for TVET colleges that consider implementing such an intervention. It means they will have to contract an external organisation to manage this type of intervention. While it is a relatively simple intervention to roll out, it does require that the implementing organisation familiarises itself with the college, especially the courses and the student culture. As noted earlier, the researcher visited the college often in order to observe students. Frequent visits to the college afforded the researcher with an opportunity to learn more about student culture, and so understand the context of the students better. For example, the researcher learned that students are hyper-visual, so messages needed to always contain at least one strong visual and an emoji or symbol. The use of the correct jargon (when appropriate), without sounding patronising was a critical factor for successful engagement with the students during this study.

*5.3.3 The coach in my pocket*

According to the motivation literature, motivated students actively choose to learn. In this study, students received two types of daily motivational messages. The first type was a motivational quote accompanied by a visual and the second type was, the 'hero' post, a story of someone who, despite seemingly insurmountable challenges, stuck to their goals, worked hard and was successful. The rationale behind the posts was to serve as intrinsic motivation boosts. If students could identify with the 'hero' of the post, they could believe that they too could overcome challenges and succeed. This is supported in the literature by Eccles and Wigfield's (2000) expectancy x value model, especially efficacy. They assert that efficacy is linked to a student's belief in their future achievements, rather than expectancy outcomes. The study's findings revealed that students responded overwhelmingly positively to these posts and messages.

For many students, this was the only support and motivation they received. In South Africa, due to the socio-economic conditions, many college students will be first-generation college graduates and will not necessarily receive emotional support from family, simply because they will not understand what that person is experiencing. The chat groups, via the inspirational Daily Kickstart, provided that much-needed support and self-esteem boost.

Perhaps a reason for the popularity of the motivational posts amongst students was that, by relating to the hero stories, the students could envisage they too could overcome adversity and achieve success. They believed this to be their possible future achievement.

Typically, at more affluent learning institutions, students have access to support staff, in the guise of either a coach or counsellor to help them identify their academic and career goals and discuss ways to achieve these goals. This person also provides counsel to students to help them manage stress and anxiety. In the findings of this study, one student mentions a counsellor at the TVET but indicates that they (the student) did not seek assistance from the counsellor because he looked anxious. A review of literature focused on Emerging Adulthood revealed that psychosocial support at tertiary institutions in South Africa was mostly non-existent (Van Breda, 2017). The literature also indicated that students in the Emerging Adulthood phase (like the students in this study) are particularly vulnerable to depression and anxiety (Arnett 2008). As noted in the literature, the outlook for South African youth is bleak: the youth unemployment rate is amongst the highest in the world. The living reality for many South African youth, like the majority of the students in this study, is that they come from impoverished households. It is plausible then to deduce from these factors that students would probably experience anxiety regarding their future in an uncertain job market, post-college. These motivational posts then served as a form of virtual coaching, encouraging students to believe in themselves. This virtual form of psychosocial support was welcomed and highly anticipated by the students in this study. Perhaps this was the reason that on the one (and only) day when the motivational message was not sent to the class, students reached out to check in with the facilitator and ask if the posts had stopped indefinitely. It was also interesting that they reached out individually, and not within the group chat, perhaps not wanting to show just how much the inspirational messages meant to them as individuals.

Aside from checking in every day with a positive motivational quote or story, the findings also noted that during exam time, extra attention was given to students, in the form with good wishes ahead of exams and post-exam check-ins. The value of 'checking in 'on the student as a 'whole person' cannot be underestimated and is supported in the literature. Van Breda (2017) discusses how most academic institutions fail to take on what he calls the psychosocial vulnerability of students and only focus on academic challenges. None of the mlearning case studies explored in the literature featured the use of a psychosocial mechanism. This lack of focus on psychosocial support for students again speaks to Van Breda's (2017) assertion that far too often in designing learning programmes, the focus is on the academic "side" of a student, with little to no regard given to the emotional "side". This study demonstrates that the use of simple motivational messages and stories can not only bolster intrinsic motivation but also provide students with a positive support mechanism.

When designing the mlearning intervention, the researcher considered how students engage with their curriculum content outside the classroom. Challenges were thus based on real-life scenarios that required students to conduct further research and apply critical thinking to the course content. Completion of the challenges was also incentivised by rewards. The findings indicate that the challenges were popular amongst the students. However, challenges were popular for different reasons. Some students enjoyed participating in the challenges because they relished in being tested and finding a solution.

Motivational theory was one of the theories framing this study, and as discussed earlier (Chapter 2), there are two types of motivation, namely intrinsic and extrinsic. Woolfolk (2013) describes intrinsic motivation as motivation that resides within a person because they find the task or activity satisfying, and they are not driven by the promise of a reward for the completion or the fulfilment of a task or activity (which is extrinsic). Student P5 thus seems to have been intrinsically motivated by the challenges because there is no reference to the challenge rewards in the student's response; instead, it appears that some students like P5 achieved a sense of fulfilment from solving the challenge. According to Deci and Ryan (2000), people with high intrinsic motivation tend to "seek out novelty and challenges, to extend one's capacities, to explore, and to learn" (p.70).

The lecturer, however, seemed to think that the rewards drove students' "hyper" response to the challenges. Incentivisation using rewards to complete a task is known as extrinsic motivation. While students never explicitly stated that they only participated in the challenges because of the rewards, they did reference the rewards in the interviews, referring to the prizes on offer as "cool."

It was interesting to note in the findings that the participation in the challenges of one class dropped substantially after one student won back to back challenges, and so won the rewards for both challenges. This finding suggests the rewards drove the participation in the challenges of students in that class. When it seemed that the rewards were "unattainable" to all students, because of the perceived domination of one student, their participation and interest in the challenges decreased. This is what Deci, Koestner, and Ryan, 1999 (as referenced in Deci & Ryan, 2000) found in their meta-analysis, i.e. that when people are motivated solely based on rewards, or the expectation of being rewarded, it undermines intrinsic motivation.

Another finding of the study indicated that students responded positively to the content they received. Content sent to students included bite-sized chunks of curriculum revision content, industry news, career and study techniques. While the college has its learning management system (LMS) called Blackboard, which is freely available to all students, less than 5% of the participants indicated that they made use of the system. In the literature on mobile learning in emerging economies, access to information is listed as one of the chief benefits of using mobile for learning. The Rumie tablet roll-out across seven countries yielded impressive results in terms of improvement in learners' academic results. And while these tablets mainly operate offline, large volumes of content are stored on it, allowing the user to access it at any time (Moon et al., 2016). Mobile learning's affordance of access to content cannot be underestimated. Students like P5, in this study, especially appreciated the revision content, *which they indicated helped them to study and revise their work, without knowing that they were doing that at the time. They recalled a specific exam instance where they remembered the answer to a question, by recalling a post in the WhatsApp group.*

Another learning theory cited in the literature, Information Processing theory, asserts that students process new information like a computer (Mayer, 1996). Students using mobile technology do not necessarily have to retain all the information sent to them because they have devices that can hold the information. However, this study employed 'chunking' the content into bite-sized parts. Students were sent these chunks at different periods, repeating the same set of chunks every few days to aide its storage in first their short and then their long-term memory. This is possibly what student P5 was referring to – the information retrieved during the exam was stored in her long-term memory. In the case studies examined in the literature, there is no evidence of other mlearning programmes using information processing theory, and specifically, chunking as was used in this study.

The self-determination theory asserts that, in order to grow and for personal well-being, people are driven by three needs: competence, relatedness (feeling included) and autonomy (Deci & Ryan, 2008). Students, who participated in this study and engaged with the content, participated in the challenges perhaps were trying to fulfil their innate need to feel competent, included and autonomous when engaging in and with this mlearning platform (Deci & Ryan, 2008). Moreover, the psychologists contend that if the students' needs were met (in this instance, using this WhatsApp group), their intrinsic motivation would be sustained. One of the findings that answered the question 'What contributory factors led to the students' successful use of mtech?' was student competence with technology. This finding cannot be undermined. If these students did not know how to use mobile technology - either their mobile phones or WhatsApp, then it would have served as a hurdle to student adoption and retention. Student P6 expressed relief that they understood how to use the WhatsApp technology because of prior experience and understood the dynamics of WhatsApp groups. It can thus be argued that this mlearning intervention, fulfilled all the processes necessary for self-determination, in much the same way that coaches help people increase their self-determined motivation. Coaches also help with an improvement in the overall well-being of their clients through autonomy-supportive behaviour (Rocchi, et al., 2013). Students in this case study were allowed to participate and leave when they chose, so they had autonomy (greater elaboration on this in the next section). Being part of these WhatsApp groups gave students a sense of community and belonging (as noted earlier, a CoP formed), meeting the requirement for relatedness. Furthermore, as noted in the finding, they all demonstrated and enjoyed using technology, thus showing competence over the technology.

*5.3.4. Mlearning gives students greater agency*

Before commencement of the WhatsApp group formation, Lecturer 1 expressed frustration at the attitude of students toward their coursework. The lecturer felt that students had low self-agency, always waiting for the lecturer to post notes and never seeking the answers themselves, or showing initiative concerning their field of study or what they would do post-college. These sentiments, from one of the lecturers (L1), during a check-in, seemed to be a commonly held perception of students amongst many lecturers working in the college. However, the findings of this study refute that view. All students interviewed were positive about their learning experience using their mobile phones and how it had assisted them during the period of study. Furthermore, they were excited that mlearning was explored as a viable supplementary tool for educational purposes. From the very high sign-up and retention rates to the high on-platform engagement rate, students seemed anything but disinterested in their learning. In the findings, this enthusiasm for learning was noted in the onboarding of students, when additional students asked to be added to the group after the initial intake. These students were absent when the researcher presented the study. Of the 50 students that signed up (including an additional four students), the retention rate was 72% (36 of the 50), with students dropping off at various times during the study. Furthermore, as noted in the findings, there were high levels of engagement during the study.

Employers often regard TVET colleges, and by extension, the TVET graduates, with disdain. This assertion, made by the Acting Director in the Department of Higher Education and Training (DHET), was based on meeting she had with prospective employers. Many employers felt that the TVET curriculum was outdated, lecturers were far removed from the labour market and many did not understand the demands of the workplace. This assertion is supported by business, which recently reinforced the view that TVET colleges do not adequately prepare students for the workplace or how to navigate life after college (Cohen, 2019). But TVET colleges have implemented policies to overcome this barrier. At False Bay College students have allotted time in their weekly schedules to attend compulsory Work Based Experience (WBE) sessions.  WBE is the practical component of students' studies. Students receive the necessary exposure to a workplace aligned to their field of study. Here the students are confronted with real-life crisis and experience the rigours of their field of study and have to apply their theoretical knowledge. That is the thinking behind the WBE session. However, in practice, this was not happening. The findings support this: students complained that their WBE sessions did not contribute to their understanding of the industry, nor did it deliver an opportunity to apply theory learned in class. Many students, like P3, felt the sessions were a waste of time, and in many cases, there was a misalignment between the WBE and field of study. Student P3 also voiced dread about attending their WBE session because of the staff's attitude towards them. Student P3 expressed their disappointment about the WBE. Instead of it being a fulfilling and enriching experience for the students, many were left unsupervised and treated poorly by the employers. Students were angry that this WBE did not enrich their lives, indicating that they did not learn much.

As discussed in the section earlier, which detailed external facilitation and SMEs, students enjoyed these interactions with industry experts and capitalised on any opportunities that presented itself. This included internships and industry meetups. Students also took the time to prepare before the group discussions with the SMEs. This high take-up, coupled with greater agency shown by students towards this mlearning intervention, is discussed in the literature and echoed earlier in this chapter and the findings. As noted in the findings, students regarded the mlearning initiative as a novel, because they had never before used WhatsApp in this way, i.e. to learn, and found it enhanced for their learning. As discussed in the previous section, the students felt a great sense of autonomy, as they could leave the group when they wanted to, and participation in the groups did not affect their grades. Deci and Ryan (2008) stated that this intrinsic motivation increases as autonomy increases. By giving students greater autonomy over their learning, their enjoyment of learning increases, which increases their desire to want to learn more.

In this study, students also relied on external experts (SMEs and the facilitator) to help them construct knowledge. Anything they could not learn on their own, or from and with their peers, they checked with these two external sources. It was evident in the findings, from the language used when addressing these two sources, that the students trusted and held them in high regard, so would want to model their (the students') endeavours on the advice and input from the experts. This is supported in the literature by Vygotsky (1978), who calls these external sources 'More Knowledgeable Others' (MKOs). The role of MKOs is critical in helping students fill in the gaps of knowledge that they may have regarding their field of study or work experience. This new knowledge is called Zone of Proximal Development (ZPD). In this study, students demonstrated that they were comfortable taking control of their learning and finding appropriate assistance. Again, counter to what the lecturer had indicated in the interview about students not wanting to take ownership of their learning and acquiring new knowledge, these students demonstrated that, given an enabling environment, this would be the stimulus for ZPD. This, therefore, implies that applications in future mlearning initiatives should have MKOs readily available so students can seek them out to help resolve the gaps in their knowledge.

Through these online interactions, students also demonstrated communication competency and character qualities such as curiosity and initiative which form part of the critical 21$^{st}$ century skills highlighted by the World Economic Forum (see Figure 1 in the literature review). Examples from the findings to support this claim include students taking the initiative to ask for internship opportunities from SMEs, as well as spending time preparing questions for their SME discussions. The implications of these findings show us that these TVET students already possess some of the critical skills needed to thrive in the job market of the 21st century. They were comfortable taking control of their education and learning. For them, information is always accessible, and they will seek out real-time information using their most treasured device, their mobile phones. This is supported in the literature: constructivist learning theory asserts that students are actively involved in their learning and knowledge construction, linking new information with existing information. The Generation Z Report (2018) also  supports this assertion, stating that GenZers respond well to and actively seek out experiences and opportunities to co-create. These young people are also comfortable collaborating with and learning from their peers. These students now need the TVET colleges and educational leaders to catch up in terms of innovating their lectures and restructuring the curriculum in ways that can best reach these digital natives.

*5.3.5 The power of connectivity*

In a pre-study survey (figure 4), 87% of students indicated that they used WhatsApp to communicate with family and friends daily, while 56% of students said they used their phones to access social media, including Facebook and Instagram. This was not the finding though during (observations) and after (interviews) the period of study. Students indicated that data costs were a barrier to accessing social media sites, and during the study, they requested that the researcher not use those channels to post clues. More than half of the students interviewed specifically referenced use of one mobile network operator, Cell C, because of its cost-effective data packages. Data costs as a barrier for use was not mentioned in any of the mobile learning case studies referenced. In their reviews of mlearning programmes, O'Hagan (2012) and Roberts (2015) do, however, reference extensive use of the Mxit platform. Perhaps indirectly, they were indicating that data costs play a role in the success of an mlearning programme. Mxit was known for having low data costs and was, therefore, an ideal platform through which to deliver educational content. Dietrich et al. (2014) tested the use of social media (Facebook) to improve contact time between students and lecturers in South Africa. Their findings did not specifically refer to data costs as being a barrier for use by students in their respective studies. However, South Africa's exorbitant data costs was revealed elsewhere in the literature. The Research ICT Africa African Mobile Pricing (RAMP) Index found that thanks to the dominance of two mobile network operators (MNOs), MTN and Vodacom, South Africans' cheapest 1GB prepaid data bundle was seven times more expensive than in Egypt.

If the supply-side is dominated by two MNOs, then consumers will pay the (steep) price. This high explains why students in the study made specific mention of Cell C as their preferred MNO. The packages offered were more competitive than the other two MNOs. How does South Africa then harness the power of connectivity if it is hamstrung by the steep cost of data? This study's definition of mlearning presupposes connectivity. It is the only way that the affordances offered by mlearning can be realised. The findings of this study show that students' appetite for mlearning is great. These digital natives want to actively contribute to their learning through content creation, as well as content consumption. Education leaders considering the rollout of any mlearning programme must factor in sensitivity around data costs. In the literature on mlearning case studies, in the Philippines, the award-winning Text2Teach programme is a great example of a public-private partnership between multiple stakeholders, that owes much of its success to the inclusion of the country's biggest MNO, Globe Telecom. Another example of the important role that MNOs play in the success of mlearning is the Nokia Maths programme in South Africa. MTN and Cell C "zero-rated" the portal, thus allowing free access for students to the maths material (Roberts et al., 2015). At the time of the study, False Bay College was considering the rollout of WiFi at its campuses, but there were concerns about misuse. This, of course, can be easily remedied by tokens and capping each student's daily usage. If connectivity challenges due to data costs persist in South Africa, the implications are dire. Students are then rendered passive vessels for receipt of information from their lecturers, instead of being able to actively construct their knowledge. If education leaders in South Africa wish to roll out the use of mlearning across colleges, then discussions with the country's MNOs must include a call for zero-rating of all educational programmes.

## 5.4 Limitations

The results of this qualitative case study cannot be generalised and applied to all TVET college students in South Africa. It was based on engagement with students attending one TVET college in the Western Cape over a limited period. This researcher did try to expand her reach of participants in the study by working with two diverse student cohorts: participants were enrolled in different study streams and different years of study. The N5 Travel and Tourism students were older and already experienced in college life, with one year of study completed by the time the researcher met them. The other group, the N4 Hospitality Management Studies students were younger, first-year college students. However, because they attended the same TVET college, they may have been influenced by the same or similar styles of lecturing or class environments and college cultures. Findings from this case study were not intended to be generalised to other student populaces.

There were also limitations regarding the scope and time of the research. The researcher could have gained more in-depth insight into students' experiences and understanding of mlearning if the study was carried out for a more extended period and included more students. Perhaps tracking students' progression through the course of one full academic year would yield different findings. It is possible that at the start of a new academic year, students are excited and eager to prove themselves, and deliver excellent results, versus closer to the end of the year, which is when this study took place.

Due to the limited time of the lecturers, the focus of the study was only on the participating students, but the study would have been further enriched if TVET lecturers were also included more formally. Therefore, if more features were revealed to the students, the lecturers would be able to track how students reacted in class, if at all. In this study, due to their work schedules, the researcher had limited access to the lecturers and was confined to unstructured interviews (as noted in Chapter 3). Furthermore, the researcher did not check in with the lecturers regularly to let them know what challenges were taking place, or what content was shared with the students. Obviously, for the sake of confidentiality, this would always exclude discussions of individual students' engagement in the WhatsApp groups.

This study only focused on the qualitative data but could be further enhanced to include quantitative measures, like the impact on student performance. However, this was curtailed by the limited time and scope of this study. It would have been interesting to have a mixed-methods study conducted over a more extended period, with the participation of the lecturers playing a more significant role. Students could then be separated by year and stream of study, into a control group, and an experimental group. Furthermore, if more time and resources were available, this could have been extended across campuses, and possibly regions.

Students in this study knew that their participation was voluntary and that this did not affect their scores. This was made explicit during the onboarding process by the researcher and later reiterated by the lecturers. Most students opted to join the WhatsApp groups and were free to leave whenever they wanted to. However, for the interviews, students volunteered, so the seven students self-selected. There is a likelihood that those seven students may have been biased positively to the study. The students in this study were all young, all in their twenties. GenZers are comfortable with technology and most grew up with the flicker of a mobile or computer screen. The researcher did not study the students who did not participate in the research. The study may have been enriched by including non-participating students, and this could have further contributed to a deeper understanding of mlearning's contribution to learning enhancement.

The researcher conducted semi-structured interviews with each of the seven student participants. The questions were open-ended, in order to gain an in-depth understanding and to encourage students to share their learning experiences while being mindful that they could feel intimidated by the fact that they were participating in research. The possible drawback is that self-reported data has been shown to be biased and to not accurately portray respondents' feelings or thoughts (van de Mortel, 2008). More research focused on students' experience using mlearning will improve educational leaders' understanding of the use of mobile technology for learning enhancement and expand the available literature.

## 5.5 Recommendations for Future Research

This exploratory case study focused on the learning experience of students enrolled at one TVET college based in the Western Cape. Reviewing the data collected using a framework that was informed by learning theory, mobile learning theory, motivational theory and various case studies detailing mobile learning programmes and projects, the following areas are recommended for further research: mlearning as a tool to foster inclusivity and personalisation of mlearning. Since this study was only based on the mlearning experiences of a group of students located at one TVET college, future research could be conducted with a representative sample of TVET students across South Africa. This would ensure that the results are generalisable.

In this study, students engaged positively within the groups, connecting with peers and the facilitator daily, thereby creating a Community of Practice. It emerged in the findings that this

CoP fostered cultural and language inclusivity, even though this was not the explicit focus of the mlearning intervention. How virtual CoPs can foster greater inclusivity of students ranging from differences in abilities, sexual orientations, ethnicities, etc. can be a beneficial research topic, especially with the focus on students who are unable to attend classes because they are physically challenged. The Communities of Practice that emerged from the two student WhatsApp groups show the effective use of mlearning as a means to foster inclusivity across cultural and language differences.

Another recommendation for future research is for an exploration of the personalisation of mlearning tools used by students. This generation has grown up accustomed to personalisation and customisation (Fluxtrends, 2018). They are accustomed to being able to customise and personalise everything from their meals and shoes to their mobile phones. As this study demonstrates, these students had a high propensity to learn from each other, the facilitator and SMEs. They responded positively to the content, motivational messages and SME discussions. Far from being the passive recipients of information, they showed a great appetite to learn and to direct that learning. However, personalisation can be costly and may affect scalability, as resources needed are far greater than a one-size-fits-all approach to learning, as is the case in the current study. The findings highlighted how students used this mobile learning that took place using WhatsApp as their coach. Further exploration of how further personalisation can work and what it will mean for learning needs to be explored and can be beneficial to educational leaders who are trying to understand how best to implement mobile technology in colleges.

While this study focused on an mlearning intervention outside of formal learning in the classroom, it would be beneficial if the focus of future research formally included mlearning. This can be done by tracking and measuring the impact of mlearning on academic achievements and the results of students. Consequently, this requires linking the content to what was covered in class on a particular day and then quizzing students on it at random intervals to check that they understand the terminology and by then measuring how they perform in formal tests based on the same content.

In this study, incentives were used to bolster students' extrinsic motivation. Students were enticed to participate in the challenges because of the rewards offered. Future research could delve deeper into the role of external rewards and could perhaps further enhance it by gamifying the mlearning, and then measuring if and how this affects students' learning.

## 5.6 Conclusion

In the Ernest Hemmingway novel, *The Sun Also Rises*, there is a dialogue that highlights the need to be agile and innovative.

*"How did you go bankrupt? Bill asked.*

*"Two ways," Mike said. "Gradually and then suddenly."*

The digital era is here, and the world has already borne witness to the effects of living in a networked society. Globally, we have seen the downside of technology's impact on jobs, as increasingly, especially within manufacturing, automation has resulted in widespread job loss. However, its positive effects: in the medical field, with 3D organ printing, and the use of drone deliveries for the transport of medication to people located in rural or remote areas. In this era of disruption, it is innovation and agility that will propel us forward. This is especially applicable to the education sector. If South Africa is to take advantage of its youth bulge and at the same time stem the tide on youth unemployment, we need to rethink how we educate young people, especially at TVET colleges. Much has been written about how these institutions hold great promise to impact youth unemployment. Not all South African youth can access university and TVET helps young people to gain work experience as part of their studies, thus alleviating the issue that many young university graduates face of having "no experience" (Lishiva, 2019). South Africa is the birthplace of a slew of mobile tech innovations, like the instant messenger service Mxit and numerous mlearning platforms and tools listed in the literature review. The time is right for educational leaders to explore how to capitalise this ubiquitous technology to improve the education and learning experience of young people, especially those at TVET colleges.

In this exploratory study, the researcher sought to understand how TVET students within this single case study used and experienced mlearning. Fifty students participated in the WhatsApp group discussions, and seven students volunteered to be interviewed. The data analyses led to five major conclusions, namely, external facilitation of the mlearning intervention fostered greater trust and use; mlearning gives students greater agency over their learning, which suggested areas for further research. These included greater personalisation and the use of an mlearning CoP to foster greater inclusivity, especially concerning students who are differently-abled or who feel excluded because of their difference to the student populace as a whole.

This study's findings are important to the academic body of knowledge because it offers an understanding of how TVET college students in an emerging economy context, experience and use mlearning. It indicates that TVET college students have a great appetite for learning and are comfortable with taking ownership of their learning if provided with support and motivation. This finding is in sharp contrast to the prevailing discourse around TVET students being unmotivated and disinterested in their future careers. As indicated in Chapter 2, there is and has been a great focus in research on how mlearning programmes, most of which were pilots that studied mlearning in a secondary education context, could be rolled out across the country. However, there is little to no understanding of how TVET students are using mlearning, and how this can be rolled out and supported, despite global attention on this subject.

As research for this study unfolded, the researcher kept in contact with the TVET college and its principals and they requested that the findings of this exploration be shared with them once the research was completed.
 False Bay College and specifically its principals, lecturers and other support staff indicated a strong desire to utilise technology to enhance learning for their students. Like other colleges and places of tertiary education, they are grappling with how to utilise technology in a way that is not only value-adding. The educators are not only concerned about the value offering technology for students while they attend college, but also beyond the walls of the college, when the students start working. Furthermore, they are concerned about the cost implications. This study highlights and addresses these concerns.

Emanating from a communication and technology background, and a deep-rooted passion for education and learning, the researcher embarked on this study determined to see how, within a resource-scarce environment, technology could be used to enhance learning from the perspective of the students. Having worked on the team that developed and launched South Africa's first virtual high school, Ukufunda, the researcher's curiosity to see how young people enrolled in tertiary institutions experienced learning using mobile technology led to this study. Peter Diamandis, executive chairman of Singularity University, wrote, "Technology is a resource-liberating mechanism. It can make the once scarce the now abundant." This is the core of inclusive innovation, as defined in Chapter 1 of this study, i.e. affordable, sustainable, accessible, and focused on improving the lives of people. The purpose of the research was to determine how mlearning can enhance and thereby support student learning outside of a formal setting, i.e. the classroom. It was established that learning with mobile technology already owned by, and thus familiar to the students, does enhance their learning.

It was a privilege to work alongside the students and lecturers at this TVET college and to explore how we can use ubiquitous technology like the mobile phone for learning. The role that education has played in my life and the lives of others who have grown up in a resource-constrained environment similar to those of the students in this study is invaluable in terms of positively changing the trajectory of our lives, and its value cannot be overstated. Embarking on this study afforded this researcher with the opportunity to explore and expand personal learning in this sphere. It appears that mlearning on its own is not the great panacea for all of South Africa's education problems, but it forms a critical part of the conversation to reform learning methods and education as the 21st century rolls on. An imagined new world of learning needs to heed the words of futurist, Alvin Toffler (Stanford, 2002): "The illiterate of the 21st century will not be those who cannot read and write, but those who cannot learn, unlearn and relearn".

## References

Afzal, Malik, M. E., Begum, I., Sarwar, K., & Fatima, H. (2012). Relationship among education, poverty and economic growth in Pakistan: An econometric analysis. *Journal of Elementary Education, 22*(1), 23-45.

Alexander, P.A. (1996). The past, present, and future of knowledge research: A re-examination of the role of knowledge in learning and instruction, *Educational Psychologist, 31*(2), 89-92, doi: 10.1080/00461520.1996.10524941

Ambrose, S., Bridges, M., DiPietro, M., Lovett, M., & Norman, M. (2010). *How learning works.* San Francisco: Jossey-Bass.

Arnett , J. J. (2000). Emerging Adulthood, a theory of development from the late teens through the twenties. *American Psychologist , 55*(5), 469-480.

Bandura, A. (1971). *Social Learning Theory.* New York City: General Learning Press.

Bandura, A. (1977). *Social Learning Theory.* Prentice Hall.

Bernard, R. (1988). *Research methods in cultural anthropology.* Beverly Hills: Sage.

Braun, V., & Clarke, V. (2006). Using thematic analysis in psychology. *Qualitative Research in Psychology, 3*(2), 77-101.

Braun, V., & Clarke, V. (2012). Research designs: Quantitative, qualitative, neuropsychological, and biological. In H. Cooper, P. Camic, D. Long, A. Panter, D. Rindskopf, & K. Sher, *APA handbook of research methods in psychology.* Washington D.C.: American Psychological Association.

Branson , N., Hofmeyr, C., Papier, J., & Needham, S. (2015). Post-school education: Broadening alternative pathways from school to work. *South African Child Gauge*, 1, 1-8.

Breda, A. D. (2017). Students are humans too:psychosocial vulnerability of first-year students at the University of Johannesburg. *South African Journal of Higher Education, 31*(5), 246-262.

Brende, B. (2015, July 7). *Why education is the key to development.* [World Economic Forum] Retrieved from https://www.weforum.org/agenda/2015/07/why-education-is-the-key-to-development/

Brinkmann , S., & Kvale , S. (2014). *Interviews learning the craft of qualitative research Interviewing.* Thousand Oaks, California: Sage.

Brown, T. H. (2003). *The role of mlearning in the future of elearning in Africa.* Paper presented at the 21st International Council for Open and Distance Education (ICDE), June, Hong Kong.

Cetinkaya, L. (2017). The impact of Whatsapp use on success in education process. *International Review of Research in Open and Distributed Learning, 18*(7). Retrieved from https://doi.org/10.1016/j.compedu.2013.08.012

Cloete, N. & Butler-Adam, J. (2012). Introduction. In H. Perold, N. Cleote & J. Papier (Eds.), *Shaping the future of South Africa's youth* (pp. 1-2). Somerset West, SA: African Minds.

Cochrane, T., & Bateman, R. (2010). Smartphones give you wings: Pedagogical affordances of mobile Web 2.0. *Australasian Journal of Educational Technology, 26*(1), 1-14. https://doi.org/10.14742/ajet.1098

Cochrane, T. (2013) A Summary and Critique of M-Learning Research and Practice. In Z. Berge, & L. Muilenberg (Eds). *Handbook of Mobile Learning.* (pp. 24-34). doi: 10.13140/RG.2.1.3259.8488

Cooper, Donald R & Schindler, Pamela S (2006). *Business research methods* (9th ed). McGraw-Hill Irwin, Boston.

Cowan, N. (2000). The magical number 4 in short-term memory: A reconsideration of mental storage capacity. *Behavioral and Brain sciences, 24*(1), 87-185. Retrieved from doi:10.1017/S0140525X01003922

Cresswell, J. (2018). *Research design: Qualitative, quantitative, and mixed methods approaches.* (5th edition. International student edition).Thousand Oaks, California: SAGE Publications, Inc..

Crotty, M. (1998). *The foundations of social research.* St Leonards: Sage.

DeMarrais, K., & Lapan, S. (2004). Qualitative interview studies: Learning through experience. In K. DeMarrais , *Foundations for research* (pp. 51-68). New Jersey: Erlbaum.

Denzin, N., & Lincoln, Y. (2003). *Strategies of qualitative inquiry* (2nd ed.). (p. 7). Thousand Oaks, CA ;: Sage.

Department of Trade & Industry. (2018, August 28). Codes of good practice on Broad Based Black Economic Empowerment: *Statement 000: Youth Employment Services.*South Africa: Pretoria. Government Printers: Department of Trade & Industry.

Department of Education. (2008). *Student support services framework.* Pretoria. Department of Education.

Department of Higher Education and Training (DHET). (2013). White Paper for post-school education and training. *Building and expanded, effective and integrated postschool system*. Pretoria, Gauteng, South Africa.

Dewey, J. (1929). *Experience and nature*. [George Allen & Unwin]. Retrieved from https://archive.org/details/experienceandnat029343mbp/page/n179/mode/2up

Dzvapatsva, G. P., Mitrovic, Z., & Dietrich, A. D. (2014). Use of social media platforms for improving academic performance at Further Education and Training colleges. *SA Journal of Information Management. 16*(1), 1-7.

Elkind, D. (1968, May 26). Giant in the Nursery - Jean Piaget. *The New York Times*. New York, United States: New York Times.


Ericsson (2012). *The Future of Learning, Networked Society* [Video file]. Retrieved from https://www.youtube.com/watch?v=quYDkuD4dMU&feature=youtu.be

Etikan, Musa & Alkassim, 2016.Comparison of Convenience Sampling and Purposive Sampling. *American Journal of Theoretical and Applied Statistics.* Vol. 5, No. 1, pp. 1-4. doi: 10.11648/j.ajtas.20160501.11

Fluxtrends. (2018). *Generation Z Report.* (2018). Pretoria, SA: Fluxtrends.

Francis, T., & Hoefel, F. (2018, November). *'True Gen': Generation Z and its implications for companies*. McKinsey & Company. Retrieved from: https://www.mckinsey.com/industries/consumer-packaged-goods/our-insights/true-gen-generation-z-and-its-implications-for-companies

Gentles, S. J., Charles, C., Ploeg, J., & McKibbon, K. (2015). Sampling in Qualitative Research: Insights from an Overview of the Methods Literature. *The Qualitative Report, 20*(11), 1772-1789. Retrieved from https://nsuworks.nova.edu/tqr/vol20/iss11/5

Gill, J., & Johnson, P. (2002). *Research methods for managers.*London: Sage.

Gillham, B. (2005). *Research interviewing the range of techniques.* Maidenhead: Open University Press.

Global System for Mobile Communications (GSMA). (2010). *mLearning: A platform for educational opportunities at the base of the pyramid.* GSMA.Retrieved from https://www.gsma.com/mobilefordevelopment/wp-

content/uploads/2012/04/mlearningaplatformforeducationalopportunitiesatthebaseofth
epyramid.pdf

Graham, L., Patel, L., Chowa, G., Khan, Z., Masa, R., Mthembu, S., & Williams, L. (2019).
*Siyakha youth assets study* . Johannesburg: Centre for Social Development in Africa.

Grimus, M., Ebner, M., & Holzinger, A. (2012). Mobile Learning as a chance to enhance
education in developing countries – on the example of Ghana.

mLearn 2012 Conference Proceedings; Specht, M., Sharples, M., Multisilta, J. (Ed.),
Helsinki, Finland, p. 340-345. Retrieved from
https://www.researchgate.net/publication/256297219_Mobile_Learning_as_a_Chance
_to_Enhance_Education_in_Developing_Countries-on_the_Example_of_Ghana

Guba, E. (1990). *The Paradigm Dialog.* Newbury Park: Sage Publications.

Guba, E., & Lincoln, Y. (2005). Paradigmatic controversies, contradictions, and emerging
confluences. In N. Denzin, & Y. Lincoln, *The Sage handbook of qualitative research*
(pp. 191--215). Thousand Oaks: Sage.

Harrison, H., Birks, M., Franklin , R., & Mills, J. (2017). Case study research: Foundations
and methodological orientations. Forum Qualitative Sozialforschung / Forum:
Qualitative Social Research, 18(1). Doi: http://dx.doi.org/10.17169/fqs-18.1.2655

Hung, D. (2001). Theories of learning and computer-mediated instructional technologies.
*Educational Media International,38*(4),  283.


ICASA. (2019). (rep.). *State of the ICT Sector in South Africa - 2019 Report* (Vol. 4, pp. 1–
92). Pretoria, Gauteng.


International Telecommunication Union (ITU) (2018). *Measuring the Information Society
Report.* [United Nations] Geneva: International Telecommunication Union.

Jarvis, P., Holford, J., & Griffin, C. (2004). *The theory and practice of learning.* London:
Taylor & Francis.

Kemp, S. (2018). *Digital in 2018.* [We are Social, Hootsuite]. Retrieved from
https://wearesocial.com/blog/2018/01/global-digital-report-2018

Kemp, S. (2019). *Country report.* Retrieved from https://wearesocial.com/uk/digital-2019

Khoza, A. (2018, March 27). *Ramaphosa launches YES initiative to address youth
unemployment.* [Fin24] Retrieved from https://www.fin24.com/Economy/ramaphosa-
launches-yes-initiative-to-address-youth-unemployment-20180327

Kohn, A. (1999). Lures for learning: Why behaviorism doesn't work in the classroom. In A. Kohn, *Punished by rewards: The trouble with gold stars, incentive plans, A's, praise, and other bribes* (pp. 119-181). New York: Houghton Mifflin.

Koszalka, T., & Ntloedibe-Kuswani, G. (2010). Literature on the safe and disruptive learning potential of mobile technologies. *Distance Education, 31*(2), 139–157.

Kukulska-Hulme, A., Sharples, M., Mildrad, M., Arnedillo-Sanchez, I., & Vavoula, G. (2009). Innovation in mobile learning: A European perspective. *International Journal of Mobile and Blended Learning, 1*(1), 13-35.

Lai, C.-H., Yang, J.-C., Chen, F.-C., Ho, C., & Chan, T.-W. (2007). Affordances of mobile technologies for experiential learning: The interplay of technology and pedagogical practices. *Journal of Computer Assisted Learning, 23*(4), 326-337.

Lavrakas, P. J. (Ed.) (2008). *Encyclopedia of survey research methods* Thousand Oaks, CA: SAGE Publications, Inc. doi: 10.4135/9781412963947

Leedy, P. D., & Ormrod, J. E. (2018). *Practical research planning and design.* New York: Pearson.

Lishiva, W. (2019, February 1). Exploring FETs and TVETs as viable alternatives. *Mail & Guardian.* Retrieved from https://mg.co.za/article/2019-02-01-00-exploring-fets-and-tvets-as-viable-alternatives

Mbukusa, N. R. (2018). Perceptions of students' on the Use of WhatsApp in Teaching Methods of English as Second Language at the University of Namibia. *Journal of Curriculum and Teaching.*

Maseko, F. (2018, August 23). Adapt or die – future proofing TVET colleges for a rapidly changing world. *IT News Africa.* Retrieved from: https://www.itnewsafrica.com/2018/08/adapt-or-die-future-proofing-tvet-colleges-for-a-rapidly-changing-world/

Mayer, R. (2002). Rote versus meaningful learning. *Theory into practice, 41*(4), 226.

Maxwell, J. (2013). *Qualitative research design: An interactive approach.* Thousand Oaks: Sage

Merriam, S. B. (1998). *Qualitative research and case study applications in education.* San Francisco: Jossey-Bass Publishers.

Merriam, S. B. (2009). *Qualitative research: A guide to design and implementation.* San Francisco: Jossey-Bass.

Merriam, S., & Tisdell, E. J. (2016). *Qualitative research: A guide to design and implementation.* Fourth edition. San Francisco: Jossey-Bass.

Mertens (1998). Research Methods in Education and Psychology: Integrating Diversity with Quantitative and Qualitative Approaches. Thousand Oaks: Sage.

Miller, G. (1956). The magical number seven, plus or minus two: Some limits on our capacity for processing information. *The Psychological Review*. *63*(2), 81–97 " https://doi.org/10.1037/h0043158

Moon, Kavanagh, Jeffrey, Gebbels & Korsgaard, (July 2016). Paper presented at International Society for Behavioral Ecology.University of Exeter. Exeter, England.

Natividad, J. N. (2008). Summative Evaluation of the ELSA Text2Teach Project: FinalReport. Prepared by Demographic Research and Development Foundation, Inc. Palma Hall,UP Diliman, Quezon City, Philippines.

Naude, L., van den Bergh, T., & Kruger, I. (2014). 'Learning to like learning': An appreciative inquiry into emotions in education. *Social Psychology of Education*, *17*, 213-215.

Nelson, L., & Padilla-Walker, L. (2013). Flourishing and floundering in emerging adult college students. *Emerging Adulthood, 1*(1), 67–78. https://doi.org/10.1177/2167696812470938

Newton, N. (2010). *The use of semi-structured interviews in qualitative research: strengths and weaknesses.* [Academia] Retrieved from https://www.academia.edu/1561689/The_use_of_semi-structured_interviews_in_qualitative_research_strengths_and_weaknesses

Nkala, T. (2019, July 4). *4IR:* The good, the bad and the inequality gap. *Daily Maverick* Retrieved from https://www.dailymaverick.co.za/article/2019-07-04-4ir-the-good-the-bad-and-the-inequality-gap/

Northrop, D. (2018). *Mobile learning in low income countries.* International Book Bank.Retrieved from http://internationalbookbank.org/wp-content/uploads/2019/03/Mobile-Learning-in-Low-Resource-Countries-2.pdf

Ntakana, K. N. (2011, October). *The effectiveness of student support programmes at a tertiary institution: A case study of Walter Sisulu University.(Masters book,* University of Zululand, South Africa). Retrieved from http://uzspace.unizulu.ac.za:8080/xmlui/handle/10530/1074

Nzimande, B. (2017, January 12). Briefing by Minister of Higher Education and Training Dr Blade Nzimande on 'Opportunities for Matric Class 2016 in Post-School Education and Training'. [*Speech.*] Pretoria, Gauteng , South Africa.

O'Hagan, T. (2013, March). *Mobility in Education: can mobile devices support teaching and learning in South Africa?* Retrieved from Helen Suzman Foundation: https://hsf.org.za/publications/focus/focus-68/%2811%29%20T.%20OHagan.pdf

Organisation for Economic Co-operation and Development OECD. (2018). *The future of education and skills 2030.* France: OECD.

Open Textbook Library. (2012). *Principles of sociological inquiry: Qualitative and quantitative methods.* [Open Textbook Library] Retrieved from https://saylordotorg.github.io/text_principles-of-sociological-inquiry-qualitative-and-quantitative-methods/s05-03-inductive-or-deductive-two-dif.html

Oxford Learner's Dictionary (n.d.). Oxford Learner's Dictionary. Retrieved from https://www.oxfordlearnersdictionaries.com/definition/english/e-learning?q=elearning

Pachler, N., Bachmair, B., & Cook, J. (2010). *Mobile learning structures, agency, practices.* New York: Springer.

Pandor, N. (2016, October 18). Minister Pandor's opening remarks at 9th Pan African TVET Colleges Conference held in Cape Town, Western Cape, South Africa. Ministry of Higher Education and Training.

Parsons, D., & MacCallum, K. (2017). An mLearning toolset for leveraging learning theory. In R. Power, M. Ally, D. Cristol, & A. Palalas, *IAmLearning: Mobilizing and Supporting Educator Practice.* International Association for Mobile Learning. Retrieved from https://iamlearning.pressbooks.com/part/ch-6-an-mlearning-toolset/

Peng , H., Su, Y.-J., Chou, C., & Tsai, C. (2009). Ubiquitous knowledge construction: Mobile learning re-defined and a conceptual framework. *Innovations in Education and Teaching International*, 46(2), 171-183.

Pervez, S. (2014). Impact of education on poverty reduction: A co-integration analyses of Pakistan. *Journal of Research in Economics and International Finance*, 3(4),83-89.

Pew Research Center. (2018). *Internet connectivity seen as having positive impact on life in sub-Saharan Africa.Retrieved from* https://www.pewresearch.org/global/2018/10/09/internet-connectivity-seen-as-having-positive-impact-on-life-in-sub-saharan-africa/

Quinn, C. (2000). *mLearning: Mobile, wireless, In-Your-Pocket LEarning.* [Line Zine]. Retrieved from http://www.linezine.com/2.1/features/cqmmwiyp.htm

Roberts, N., Spencer-Smith, G., Vänskä, R., & Eskelinen, S. (2015). From challenging assumptions to measuring effect: Researching the Nokia Mobile Mathematics Service in South Africa. *South African Journal of Education, 35*(2)1-13.

Ryan , R., & Deci , E. (2000). Self-Determination Theory and the facilitation of intrinsic motivation, social development, and well-being. *American Psychologist,55*(1) 68-78.

Sambira, J. (2013, October). *Africa's mobile youth drive change.* [Africa Renewal]. Retrieved from https://www.un.org/africarenewal/magazine/may-2013/africa%E2%80%99s-mobile-youth-drive-change

Saunders, M., Lewis, P., & Thornhill, A. (2009). *Research Methods for Business Students.* Essex: Pearson.

Schwandt, T. A. (2007). *The SAGE dictionary of qualitative inquiry* (Vols. 1-0). Thousand Oaks, CA: SAGE Publications

Schunk, D. (2012). *Learning Theory.* Boston: Pearson.

Schunk, D., Meece, J., & Pintrich, P. (2014). *Motivation in education: Theory, research and applications.* Essex: Pearson.

Sharples, M., Taylor, J., & Vavoula, G. (2006). A Theory of Learning for the Mobile Age. *Sage*, 221-247.

Sharples, M., & Pea, R. (2014). Mobile Learning. In R. Sawyer (Ed.), *The Cambridge Handbook of the Learning Sciences* (Cambridge Handbooks in Psychology, pp. 501-521). Cambridge: Cambridge University Press. doi:10.1017/CBO9781139519526.030

Siemens, G. (2005). *Connectivism: A learning theory for the digital age.* Retrieved from International Journal of Instructional Technology and Distance Learning,: https://lidtfoundations.pressbooks.com/chapter/connectivism-a-learning-theory-for-the-digital-age/

Sobel, D. (1990, August 20). B.F. Skinner, the Champion of Behaviorism Is Dead at 86. Retrieved from https://www.nytimes.com/1990/08/20/obituaries/b-f-skinner-the-champion-of-behaviorism-is-dead-at-86.html

Sommer, M., & Dumont, K. (2011). Psychosocial Factors Predicting Academic Performance of Students at a Historically Disadvantaged University. *South African Journal of Psychology, 41*(3), 386–395. https://doi.org/10.1177/008124631104100312

Stake, R. E. (2005). *Multiple case study analysis.* New York: Guilford Press.

Stake, R. (2010). *Qualitative research: Studying how things work.* New York: The Guilford Press.

Statistics South Africa. (2019, May 14). *Quarterly Labour Force Survey – QLFS*

*Q1:2019*. [Media Release] Pretoria, South Africa: Department of Statistics South Africa.

*Sunday Times Gen Next Awards*. (2019). [The Media Online] Retrieved from
https://themediaonline.co.za/2019/06/winners-of-the-2019-sunday-times-gen-next-awards/

Taljaard, I. (2008). South Africa's youth bulge: Risk or opportunity? *Future Takes*. Future Takes, 7(1).

Tanner, J., Arnett, J., & Leis, J. (2009). Emerging adulthood: Learning and development during the first stage of adulthood. In C. Smith, & N. DeFrates-Densch, *Handbook of Research on Adult Learning and Development* (p. 34). New York: Routledge.

Thalheimer, W. (2006, February). Spacing Learning Events Over Time: What the Research Says. Retrieved June 20, 2019, http://www.work-learning.com/catalog/

Thies, M, (2018). *Boosting skills learning through mobile technology: The skills-pedagogy-technology nexus.* Paper presented at the UNESCO-UNEVOC workshop 'Managing skills in a time of disruption'. Mobile Learning Week . UNEVOC.

Tosuncuoglu , I. (2012). ESL/EFL, Technology and motivation: The Turkish case. *Journal of Emerging Trends in Engineering and Applied Sciences (JETEAS)*, *3*(4), 677-681.

Traxler, J., & Kukulska-Hume, A. (2005). Mobile learning in developing countries knowledge series. *Commonwealth of Learning. Retrieved* http://oasis.col.org/bitstream/handle/11599/77/KS2005_mlearn.pdf?sequence=1&isAllowed=y

Traxler, (2009). Learning in a Mobile Age, International Journal of Mobile and Blended Learning, 1(1), 1-12.

Traxler, J. (2018). Learning with mobiles: The Global South. *Research in Comparative and International Education*, *13*(1), 152–175https://doi.org/10.1177/1745499918761509.

Udell , C., & Woodill, G. (2014). *Mastering Mobile Learning.* New Jersey: John Wiley & Sons Inc.

UNESCO. (2012). *Turning on Mobile Learning in Africa and the Middle East.* Paris: UNESCO Working Paper Series on Mobile Learning.

UNESCO-UNEVOC. (2009). *TVETipedi* . [UNESCO-UNEVOC] Retrieved from
https://unevoc.unesco.org/go.php?q=TVETipedia+Glossary+A-Z&id=474

United Nations. (2016, August 3). *Sustainable Development Goals*. Retrieved from
https://www.un.org/sustainabledevelopment/blog/2016/08/jack-ma-quality-rural-education-key-for-china/

Van Breda, A. (2017). Students are humans too:psychosocial vulnerability of first-year students at the Universe

van de Mortel, T. (2008). *Faking it: social desirability response bias in self-report research.* Retrieved from School of Health and Human Sciences : https://epubs.scu.edu.au/hahs_pubs/2/

Viljoen, J., Du Preez, C., & Cook, A. (2005). The case for using SMS technologies to support distance education students in South Africa. *Perspectives in Education, 23l*(4),115-122.

Vygotsky, L.L.S. (1978). Mind in society: The development of higher psychological processes. Cambridge, MA: Harvard University Press.

Wenger, E. (2010). Communities of Practice and Social Learning Systems: the Career of a Concept. In C. Blackmore, *Social Learning Systems and Communities of Practice* (pp. 179-199). London: Springer London.

Whyte , A., & Tedds , J. (2011). *Making the case for research data management.* [Digital Curation Centre] Retrieved from http://www.dcc.ac.uk/resources/briefing-papers

Wigfield, A., & Eccles, J. S. (2000). Expectancy-Value Theory of Achievement Motivation. *Contemporary Educational Psychology, 25*:68-81.

Winthrop, R., & McGivney, E. (2016, May). Skills for a changing world: Advancing quality learning for vibrant societies. Center for Universal Education at Brookings.

Wolcott, H. F. (2005). *The art of fieldwork.* Walnut Creek: AltaMira Press.

Woollfolk, A. (2008). *Educational Psychology Edition 10.* San Francsisco: Pearson.

World Bank. (2016). *Exploring the relationship between broadband and economic growth.* World Bank.Retrieved from http://pubdocs.worldbank.org/en/391452529895999/WDR16-BP-Exploring-the-Relationship-between-Broadband-and-Economic-Growth-Minges.pdf

World Bank. (2018). *Overcoming poverty and inequality in South Africa.* Washington DC: The World Bank. Retrieved http://documents.worldbank.org/curated/en/530481521735906534/pdf/124521-REV-OUO-South-Africa-Poverty-and-Inequality-Assessment-Report-2018-FINAL-WEB.pdf

World Bank. (2018). *World Development Report 2018: Learning to realize education's promise.* Washington, DC: World Bank.Retrieved from https://www.worldbank.org/en/publication/wdr2018

World Economic Forum (WEF). (2015). *New Vision for education unlocking the potential of technology.* Geneva: World Economic Forum. Retrieved from http://www3.weforum.org/docs/WEFUSA_NewVisionforEducation_Report2015.pdf

Yin, R. (1994). *Case study research: Design and methods.* Thousand Oaks: Sage.

Yin, R. K. (2009). *Case study research design and methods.* (Volume 5). Thousand Oaks: Sage.

## APPENDIX

Appendix A: Pre-Observation Background Questionnaire

Appendix B: Semi-structured Student Interview Questions

Appendix C: Praxis Model

**Appendix A**
**Pre-Observation Background Questionnaire**

**How can technology enhance learning?**

You are invited to participate in the following survey, which forms part of my MPhil research.

The purpose of this survey is to gain an understanding of factors that affect the learning experience of students and their use of and understanding of technology as it relates to their learning and studies.

It should take 5-10 minutes to complete the questionnaire.

All survey responses are anonymous, and the data collected will be kept strictly confidential.

Your participation in this research is voluntary and you can choose to withdraw from it at any time.

If you have any questions with regards to the research, you can contact me, Lea-Anne Moses at the following e-mail address: leamoses@gmail.com

**Section 1: Student details**

1.1. What's your gender?

| | |
|---|---|
| **Female** | |
| **Male** | |

1.2. How old are you?

| | |
|---|---|
| 17-19 | |
| 20-22 | |
| 22-25 | |
| 25+ | |

1.3. What course are you enrolled in?

| | |
|---|---|
| Hospitality | |
| Tourism | |

**1.4. Please select your home language**

| Afrikaans | |
|---|---|
| English | |
| Xhosa | |
| Zulu | |
| Other | |

**1.5. How far do you live from the college?**

| 5km and under | |
|---|---|
| 5-10km | |
| 10-20km | |
| 20+ kms | |

**1.6. How do you commute/travel to college?**

| Public Transport | |
|---|---|
| Private car | |

**1.7. What do you do during your commute/travel?**

| Read | |
|---|---|
| Revise college work | |
| Nothing | |
| Chat | |
| Listen to music/radio | |

**1.8 What will you do once you complete your studies at college?**

| Pursue further studies | |
|---|---|
| Work | |
| Open my own business | |
| Travel | |
| Travel & work | |
| Unsure | |

**1.9 How often do you use the following social networks?**

| | Never | Very rarely (once a month or less) | Rarely (2-3 times a month) | Occasionally (2-3 times a week) | Frequently (1-2 times a day) | Very frequently (more than times a day) |
|---|---|---|---|---|---|---|
| Facebook | | | | | | |
| Twitter | | | | | | |
| Pinterest | | | | | | |

| Instagram | | | | | | |
|---|---|---|---|---|---|---|
| Youtube | | | | | | |
| Mxit | | | | | | |
| Reddit | | | | | | |

## Section 2: Cellphone usage

### 2.1. Do you own a cellphone?

| Yes | |
|---|---|
| No | |

### 2.2. If yes, what is the make and model of your cellphone?

_______________________________________________

### 2.3. If you don't own a cellphone, do you have a sim card/s that you insert in someone else's cellphone?

| Yes | |
|---|---|
| No | |

### 2.4 Do you use more than one sim card?

| Yes | |
|---|---|
| No | |

### 2.5. How much do you spend per week on airtime?

| R5 and less | |
|---|---|
| R5 – R10 | |
| R10 – R20 | |
| R20+ | |

### 2.6.  Rate the following statement
I mainly use my cellphone to

| | Very rarely (once a month or less) | Rarely (2-3 times a month) | Occasionally (2-3 times a week) | Frequently (1-2 times a day) | Very frequently (more than 2 times a day) |
|---|---|---|---|---|---|
| Make phone calls | | | | | |
| Access the internet | | | | | |
| Send instant messages (e.g. Whatsapp) | | | | | |

| | Never | Very rarely (once a month or less) | Rarely (2-3 times a month) | Occasionally (2-3 times a week) | Frequently (1-2 times a day) | Very frequently (more than 2 times a day) |
|---|---|---|---|---|---|---|
| Use social media | | | | | | |
| Email | | | | | | |

## Section 3: You and your studies

3.1 Rate the following statement by ticking the box you feel best describes your usage of the platform/service:

| | Never | Very rarely (once a month or less) | Rarely (2-3 times a month) | Occasionally (2-3 times a week) | Frequently (1-2 times a day) | Very frequently (more than 2 times a day) |
|---|---|---|---|---|---|---|
| I check the False Bay Facebook group | | | | | | |
| Use the class Whatsapp groups (if they exist) | | | | | | |
| Use Blackboard | | | | | | |
| Use the college computer lab | | | | | | |

3.2. Tick the box you feel best describes how you feel about statement:

| | Strongly Disagree | Disagree | Neither agree nor disagree | Agree | Strongly Agree |
|---|---|---|---|---|---|
| I revise for tests and exams on my own | | | | | |
| I find study groups useful to help me understand my work better | | | | | |
| I feel well informed about college services available to me | | | | | |
| I know how to access potential employers | | | | | |

| | | | | | |
|---|---|---|---|---|---|
| I make use of the college's career services | | | | | |
| I would use a mobile app for my field of study | | | | | |
| I'm positive about my future career | | | | | |
| I regard learning as fun | | | | | |
| I know how to access additional revision material provided by the college e.g. past exam papers | | | | | |
| I do additional reading and research | | | | | |
| I'm easily distracted when I study | | | | | |
| It's difficult to study at home | | | | | |

### 3.3. Describe what you will regard as success at the end of this academic year

|  |
|---|
|  |

Thank you for participating in the survey!

# Appendix B

## Semi-structured Student Interview Questions

1. Before using Whatsapp for your hospitality/tourism course, how would you describe your use of Whatsapp and other messaging apps?

2. What was it like to use Whatsapp to communicate with other students and the facilitator about your hospitality/tourism course?

3. In what ways did you use this Whatsapp group to communicate about your course?

4. How, if at all, did your use of Whatsapp to communicate about your course change during the college year?

5. Could you describe a moment during the year where using Whatsapp had an impact on you or your learning?

6. Overall, how would you describe the using Whatsapp to communicate about your hospitality/tourism course?

7. How would you describe being connected with fellow students in your course through this Whatsapp group?

8. How would you describe having access to tourism/ hospitality experts via Whatsapp for your course?

9. What benefits and drawbacks did you find in using this Whatsapp group for your course?

10. Overall, how did the use of the Whatsapp group impact your learning in your course?

11. Do you feel that using Whatsapp for your course has had a lasting impact on your learning or how you learn?

12. What other information would you like to share about using Whatsapp for your course or about your learning since then?

# Appendix C: Praxis Model

**Key Partners**

TVET Colleagues
Working Professionals
Developers
Corporates
Translators
Industry bodies

**Key Activities**

Creation of content
Delivery of content
Networking

**Key Resources**
Mobile apps
Partnerships with
industry bodies
Partnerships with
TVETs
Content providers

**Value Proposition**

Access to SMEs
Access to content
Help students with revision
and exam prep
Flexibility to assist students
at any time
Improve TVET throughput

**Customer Relationships**

TVET college info
sessions
Social Media
Mainstream media
Community townhalls

**Channels**

Mobile app
Online platform

**Customer Segmentations**

TVET students (national)
Other students
Corporates
Government departments

**Cost Structure**

Development costs and maintenance
Operations
Marketing

**Revenue Streams**

Subscriptions
Advertising revenue
Once-off purchases
CSR and marketing budgets